A SERVICE OF DEATH AND RESURRECTION

A SERVICE OF DEATH AND RESURRECTION

The Ministry of the Church at Death

SUPPLEMENTAL WORSHIP RESOURCES 7

ABINGDON
Nashville
1979

A SERVICE OF DEATH AND RESURRECTION

ISBN 0-687-38075-8

MANUFACTURED BY THE PARTHENON PRESS AT
NASHVILLE, TENNESSEE, UNITED STATES OF AMERICA

Contents

Congregational folder is inserted in the back of the book.

Preface

This volume of resources for the ministry of the church at death is the seventh in the Supplemental Worship Resources (SWR) series—originally called the Alternate Rituals series—developed and sponsored by the Section on Worship of the Board of Discipleship of The United Methodist Chuch.

When The United Methodist Church was formed in 1968, *The Book of Discipline* provided (Par. 1388) that

> The hymnals of The United Methodist Church are the hymnals of The Evangelical United Brethren Church and *The Methodist Hymnal* [later retitled *The Book of Hymns*]; the Ritual of the Church is that contained in the *Book of Ritual* of The Evangelical United Brethren Church, 1959 and *The Book of Worship for Church and Home* of The Methodist Church.

A need quickly became apparent, however, for supplemental worship resources which, while not replacing the official Ritual of the Church, would provide alternatives that more fully reflect developments in the contemporary ecumenical church. The General Conference of 1970 authorized the Commission on Worship to begin work in this area, and the General Conferences of 1972 and 1976 authorized the Board of Discipleship "to develop standards and resources for the conduct of public worship in the churches" (1976 *Book of Discipline*, Par. 1316.2). The resulting series of publications began with *The Sacrament of the Lord's Supper: An Alternate Text 1972* (SWR1), which was published both in a Text Edition and later (1975) in a Music Edition. Intensive work during the next four years led to the publication in 1976 of *A Service of Baptism, Confirmation, and Renewal: An Alternate Text 1976* (SWR 2), *Word and Table: A Basic Pattern of Sunday Worship for United Methodists* (SWR 3), and *Ritual in a New Day: An Invitation* (SWR 4). In 1973 work was begun that has now resulted in the publication of *A Service of Christian Marriage* (SWR 5) and the present volume. Further publications in this series are in preparation and will appear soon.

A Service of Death and Resurrection supplements "The Order for the Burial of the Dead" in *The Book of Worship for Church and Home,* of the former Methodist Church, and "Burial of the Dead: A Christian Funeral" in the *Book of Ritual* of the former Evangelical United Brethren Church. The introductory chapter and the commentary in the present volume illumines the use of these official rites as well as this service itself and additional resources published here. The desire of the Section on Worship is not to discourage the use of older resources but to enlarge the range of choices open to United Methodist ministers and congregations and to contribute to the ecumenical dialogue now taking place concerning the Christian funeral.

This volume, like the other publications in this series, represents the corporate work of the task force which prepared the manuscript and of the Section on Worship, acting as an editorial committee. which determined the original specifications and carefully examined and edited the manuscript before approving it for publication. Dr. Paul W. Hoon, Henry Sloane Coffin Professor Emeritus of Pastoral Theology at Union Theological Seminary in New York City, chaired the task force which produced the manuscript and was the principal writer. Other members of this task force were Dr. William K. Burns, Minister of Music at the Morrow Memorial United Methodist Church in Maplewood, New Jersey; Dr. L. L. Haynes, Jr., Pastor of Wesley United Methodist Church in Baton Rouge, Louisiana; Dr. Hoyt L. Hickman of the Section on Worship staff; and Dr. Edgar N. Jackson, United Methodist minister and author of numerous books and articles on death, grief, and the funeral. The Rev. Thom C. Jones and Dr. Carleton R. Young assisted in the preparation of musical suggestions. Dr. Ekkehard Muehlenberg of Claremont School of Theology rendered knowledgeable assistance. Dr. Peggy West of United Methodist Communications edited parts 1 and 2. General manuscript preparation was done by Dr. Hoyt L. Hickman, Everland

Robinson, Theresa Santillan, and Davelyn Vignaud in the office of the Section on Worship.

The members and staff of the Section on Worship, listed below, wish to thank the many persons who have shared with us their thoughts and their funeral and memorial services and invite all those who create or discover anything they think may be of wider interest to send such materials to the Section on Worship, PO Box 840, Nashville, Tennessee 37202. They have greatly helped us in the preparation of this volume and will make possible improved services in the years to come. We commend this volume to the use of local churches with the hope that it will be useful in the worship of God and the proclamation of the gospel of Jesus Christ.

Bishop Robert E. Goodrich, Jr., Chairperson, Section on Worship
James F. White, Chairperson, Editorial Committee
Paul F. Abel
Phyllis Close
Edward L. Duncan
Judy Gilreath
Kay Hereford
Judith Kelsey-Powell
Marilynn Mabee
L. Doyle Masters
William B. McClain
Louise H. Shown
Carlton R. Young
Philip E. Baker, Ex Officio
   representing the Fellowship
   of United Methodist Musicians
Elise M. Shoemaker, Ex Officio
   representing the United Methodist Society for Worship
Roberto Escamilla, Associate General Secretary
Hoyt L. Hickman, Assistant General Secretary
Thom C. Jones, Staff

I. The Ministry of the Church at Death

The Christian gospel is a message of death and resurrection. The very heart of Christian faith, this message is celebrated whenever Christians worship, but it addresses the Christian community with singular power when the community must deal with human death. To repossess and restate this message is a major task of the church in every generation. *A Service of Death and Resurrection* attempts to perform that task for today.

In fulfilling that purpose, the traditional funeral service is here modified and interpreted in light of two major considerations.

The first of these is the broader context of the gospel message of death and resurrection. The funeral service is treated as part of the larger process of the Christian community living out the gospel of death and resurrection, and not as an isolated rite. The Christian funeral is as much an act of corporate worship as any other worship activity; and the heart of the proclamation at a Christian funeral, as at any other Christian service, is the gospel message of death and resurrection.

The second consideration is to bring to bear on the funeral experience a range of interrelated perspectives: *theological* understanding, *pastoral* care, *liturgical* purpose, *psychological* knowledge, *cultural* and *ethnic* attitudes and practices, and *aesthetic* sensitivity. The variety among these perspectives makes for a fruitful tension; and openness to it should be understood, in part, as an effort to be faithful to the fourfold Wesleyan norms of Scripture, tradition, experience, and reason.

But more than anything else, Christian funeral services today need theological integrity and a clearer sense of identity as worship. Cultural pluralism and secularism have often denatured the Christian funeral of that which makes it

Christian. Even Christian symbol and ritual have been corrupted by commercialization or have become dull through familiarity and habit. This discussion, therefore, begins, with a treatment of the context of faith and doctrine in which the funeral should be set in order for it to be Christian.

A. The Perspective of Christian Faith

Biblical faith portrays death and resurrection in images such as Fall, Deluge, Covenant, Passover, Exodus, Promised Land, Temple, Exile, Valley of Dry Bones, Healing, and Baptism. These depict death and resurrection variously as threat and deliverance, slavery and liberation, extinction and identity, forgiveness for the past and a crossing over into a new life, brokenness and healing. The Passover-Exodus event, in particular, pervades the Old Testament and is fundamental for understanding the New Testament.

Jesus Christ in his person, his mind, his ministry, his teaching, and his saving work supremely declares the death-resurrection message. Scripture all but exhausts imagery and thought to say this. Through his conquest of death and sin, Christ as the Second Adam figures a new creation, and as Logos he incarnates the creative life of the universe. While bearing the form of God in his preexistent life, he yet humbled himself unto death and was raised as Lord that all might confess his name. In his casting out devils and healing the sick, in freeing the bound and raising the dead, the forces of life prevail over the forces of death. The truth of his teaching, which never passes away, saves from illusion and leads into eternal life. In his cross and resurrection death is destroyed, and a new heaven and a new earth have come to be. Buried and reborn with him in Baptism, the Christian is nourished by his body and blood unto everlasting life. Those who trust in him as Savior, obey him as Lord, and love one another with his love have passed from death into life. In the bearing of his cross and daily denial of self, his followers find true life. In ways that the mind cannot rationally comprehend, and only faith apprehends, he comes again to judge the living and the

12

dead. In the communion of saints, his church, the faithful living and the faithful dead are made one. Death and resurrection—upon this fugal theme the mind of the church broods in countless ways. This message is the hinge of Christian existence, the biblical verdict on the meaning and destiny of human life.

Correspondingly, this vision is the theme of Christian worship. The drama of the Christian year unfolds it. The Sunday service—a little Easter—and the pattern of daily prayer reenact it. Baptism as dying and rising with Christ sacramentally recapitulates it. The Lord's Supper re-presents it. Perhaps most directly of all, the Christian funeral proclaims it. At the most fateful moment in human experience, when the enigma of death throws us back on life's fundamental questions, the funeral liturgy declares that in the midst of life we are in death, and that beyond death there is life.

In its own way, our wider human experience also echoes this theme. Life often is characterized by diminutions that in greater or lesser degree are forms of death. Jesus' insight, that only as a grain of wheat falls into the ground and dies can life be brought forth, rings true with many nuances of meaning. Birth itself is fraught with threat and pain. The cycles of nature unfold death and resurrection for those who have eyes to see. In our psychic history, images and myths deep in our conscious and subconscious life act out this theme; and, not surprisingly, drama and story abound with it. In our social history, the struggle against the forces of evil and death, waged in the faith that "we shall overcome" and that a better life can be won for humankind, attest to it. In our moral history, the demand to sacrifice power or freedom or possessions in order that human life may be enhanced and made more just embodies it.

Similarly, personal experience testifies that one can fully affirm life only as one truthfully affirms death. To live in reality, does not this mean accepting, not escaping, the smaller deaths—the "mortifications"—the self must daily die if a more complete life is to be had? The discipline of the scientist, the sacrifices of a parent, the asceticism of the saint—are not these diminutions, accepted in hope of a richer life, which may be spoken of as a kind of resurrection? The transfiguration of suffering into meaning can sustain and nourish, even ennoble—an experience known to Christians and non-Christians alike. Does not new life in this sense depend on bearing pain that is really a partial death of the self? Is this not grief? Is not grief dying a little? And does not grief take a thousand forms? In short, grief and death mingled with new life in the funeral experience are resonant with death and life as we know them elsewhere, and the church rightly appeals to our wider experience in order better to understand its own message.

However, while biblical death and resurrection are echoed in, they are not to be equated with, our experience elsewhere; and the truth of the church's message does not finally depend upon verification by other than Christian faith. The New Testament, however its perspectives may vary in other respects, consistently underscores the reality of death and views human nature as "naturally" mortal, not immortal. Death is "enemy," not friend. Death, further, is bound up with sin. Even now, death is experienced in our lower nature that rebels against God and offends against others. The connection between death and sin cannot be set aside, if for no other reason than that people still fear death. Often this fear is deviously masked in other fears and behavioral expressions. Yet at root, it is a metaphysical and moral fear. It is anxiety before one's ultimate destiny conditioned by the moral quality of one's life, what the Bible refers to as "unfaith" and "sin." It is in this light that the Bible makes the tremendous claim that in perfect faith and love there is no fear, that those who believe and love have already passed from death into life. Abundant evidence from the Christian experience of those who have so believed and loved validates this claim.

Similarly, Christian resurrection is not to be equated with the immortality or survival to which other areas of experience appear to bear witness. Even less is Christian resurrection to be reduced to such concepts as living on in others, reincarnation as taught in other religions, or paranormal states. For one thing, immortality is a negative assertion that merely claims the soul does not die. Resurrection is a positive assertion: the person is raised to life. Further, resurrection affirms life in the "body" understood as the total matrix of personality; it does not exalt "soul" and denigrate "body" as does the concept of immortality. Also, Christian resurrection is life in community, not solitary survival of the self. Most fundamentally, Christian resurrection inheres first in God's nature, not in ours, in his power acting to raise Jesus Christ from the dead, not in our own faculties. Resurrection is a divine action, not a human deed. As such, resurrection is both future reality and present possibility. As future, it is marked by disjunction, renewal, and reorientation of life of a quality incommensurate with what we may know or are able to imagine. This in part is the meaning of Paul's contrast of the perishable with the imperishable, the terrestrial with the celestial, and of John's assertion that while we are God's children now, it does not yet appear what we shall be. Yet, the Christian is a child of God now, and resurrection to eternal life begins, not at the moment of physical death, but of spiritual birth. Thus understood, resurrection in light of the Christian gospel is a reality centered in Jesus Christ that ultimately is apprehended only through faith in him. It cannot be proved nor disproved by empirical evidence.

However, if Christian death and resurrection cannot be defined by or equated with death and resurrection as encountered elsewhere, it is still true that they may be intimated by these other experiences. Death and resurrection together appear to be too deeply written into the texture of human experience to be denied. Here human truth and Christian truth, while different, yet converge. Thus, there is a certain inevitability in the theme of death and resurrection being the theme of both the funeral service itself and of the process encompassing it.

In this process and the rites that are a part of it, people will perceive the meanings of death and resurrection unevenly, on various levels, and voice these in a multitude of ways. Their perceptions of mourners may be Christian, or only theistic or humanistic or confused or secularized. Some mourners will be unable to accept or articulate the reality of death, especially if it has come as a crushing blow; to others death will be welcome as the quiet closing of a richly fulfilled life. Some people will meet death with fear and trembling as "the last enemy" to be destroyed, while to others it will seem an answer to the prayer "Come, Sweet Death" and a joyful "going home." Indeed, the very metaphors people use or respond to will be revealing. Some will speak of death as "the great leveller," setting even the greatest of human achievements alongside the most humble. Others will regard it as the "final absurdity" in an essentially absurd world. Some will conceptualize death as "sleep" or as "gate" or as "the will of God," others as "adventure" or "riddle."

Likewise, resurrection will be variously understood. To some it will mean a fulfillment not experienced in this life, to others a ghostlike existence, to others the restoration of faculties wasted by disease, to others reunion with loved ones. To some, resurrection will mean eternal life over which sin and death no longer have dominion, to some the vision of God, to others fire and brimstone, to others graduation into a higher level of knowledge and understanding. Sometimes people will need to be helped toward resurrection faith; at other times faith is already so strong that it can immediately be the basis for praise and celebration.

People's understandings and misunderstandings, attitudes and reactions of whatever sort, will need both theological and psychological attention. The pastor must know the biblical faith and be sensitive to the people's needs and customs. This task requires bringing together the truth of Christian faith, the insights of psychology, a knowledge of the culture and of the subcultures in which we live, the social wisdom of custom and tradition, liturgical competence, and—informing all—pastoral compassion and care.

B. Death, Bereavement, Grief, and Mourning

To understand this task, four terms need to be distinguished that are often confusingly related to one another but which refer to different realities. *Death* and *bereavement* denote events in people's personal history. A person "dies," and others are thereby "bereaved." *Grief* is the emotion caused by the event. *Mourning* is the spiritual, psychological, even moral, process of coping with and working through grief, of regaining inner wholeness and balance.

Because not all deaths are the same, *death* is experienced differently, and the nature of *bereavement* varies accordingly. The death of a person who has lived a long and useful life, who may even have looked forward to dying, is a quite different event from the untimely or tragic death of a child or youth, or of one on the verge of great usefulness. The character of the resulting grief and the course of the mourning process will consequently vary.

Experience of death also varies from one period of history and from one social milieu to another. At the beginning of this century more than one-half of all deaths were among children. Currently, two-thirds of all deaths occur among people sixty-five years of age or older. Today, through the control of disease, the death of children in the United States averages only about 6 percent of all deaths, although among the impoverished it is much higher. While medical practice and changed social circumstances have modified the event of death and the ways we experience it, they have not altered its inevitability nor the confrontation with one's own mortality it brings to the living. The ways in which the bereaved handle this confrontation will of course vary. Each survivor brings to it a unique personality structure, emotional life, and religious orientation requiring pastoral sensitivity.

Whatever the nature of the death, if there are emotional ties between the deceased and the living there will be *grief*. Indeed the degree of grief will be in proportion to the strength of these ties. In recent years we have been able to define grief more fully and understand its dynamics more adequately. We have learned how profound and complex an emotion it is. We have learned its many faces—tenderness, guilt, resignation, hostility, anger, peace, dependence, feelings of injustice, sometimes a new mellowness and a new breadth of understanding, and even envy of the dead when the will to live and the will to die struggle with one another. Most essentially, grief derives from love; and because love is the dynamic joining of two beings one with the other, the merging to greater or lesser degree of self with self, pain inevitably results when part of the self is torn away. This pain—resulting from the death of one's self in another's death—is grief. Hence grief is an honorable emotion because it is the other side of the coin of love. If we never knew love, there is little chance that we would ever know grief.

We have also learned much about grief from research in psychosomatic medicine, which investigates the reciprocal effect that emotions and the physical body exert upon each other. Emotional states produce physical responses, and bodily conditions produce emotional responses. Implicit in this research is the promise that much health and illness are organic behavior, the body positively and negatively acting out its deepest feelings. Predictably, an emotion as deep as acute grief can affect virtually every body system. Thus, those who grieve should not consider themselves abnormal if they experience loss of appetite, nausea, irregularities in breathing, choking, weakness, unsteadiness, loss of muscular control, frequent crying, dryness in the mouth or eyes. People can be helped by knowing that grief can temporarily produce quite profound changes in their bodies.

Acute grief may also manifest itself in attitudes toward God, toward other people, toward life. Religious faith no less than other attitudes is emotionally, even physically, conditioned. Doubt, depression, even despair are not uncommon. These are usually of limited duration because the momentum of life and the will to believe forged in previous experience tend to move us through them. Personal relationships may also be affected. The grieving person may become irritable, critical of others, overly sensitive to things said or unsaid, done or not done. When this happens, those who grieve should be taught to be kind to themselves and not judge themselves harshly because these feelings, too, will likely pass. However, if they do not, if a structural change of personality and attitudes persists for a substantial time, intensive counseling or psychotherapy may be called for.

The working through of grief called *mourning* requires a greater or lesser period of time, depending on circumstances. Estimates vary from six weeks to several months. Occasionally, the mourning necessary to restored health—physical, emotional and spiritual—may take years. Psychologically understood, mourning is the gradual repair of the psychic wound dealt to the personality by death; the letting go of the dead part of the self and the formation, as it were, of new psychic tissue; the righting of the personality's vital balance that has temporarily been thrown into disequilibrium by destruction of part of the self.

As such, mourning must be expected to engage a person's total being. The finality of the death event needs to be inwardly appropriated and the pain of severing felt. Finitude—that is, the end of something, the ceasing to be, the awareness that the human person belongs to time and can be annihilated—must be experienced in its threat and then transcended. The self's vital energies must be removed, emotional investment in the lost object withdrawn and then redirected. Orientation toward the deceased as part of the source of the mourner's identity, and dependence upon the deceased as source of the mourner's security, have to be relinquished and new centers of psychic reference found. All this of course does not mean that the mourner ceases to love the person who has died. Rather, in emotionally letting go, the work of mourning can give back the deceased in a way that physical circumstance can never again disrupt.

However, because mourning involves dealing with the shock of finitude in an emotionally charged way, it raises anew the question of what is permanent and what is transient. It imposes the strain of stating afresh the meanings one believes are worth living for. It causes reappraisal of the values from which one had supposed one had drawn life. It compels a new decision as to where security ultimately lies. Similarly, mourning prompts the review of the survivors' past attitudes and behavior toward the deceased. Mourning exposes the poverty or the fullness with which love answered love. The sense of what religion calls sins of commission and omission is rekindled. Affirmation or rejection become understood again for what they are.

Now, these are religious and moral matters, indeed even philosophical and theological ones. Hence, mourning understood as resurrection from a kind of death into a new quality of life must be comprehended in both religious and psychological ways. In particular, Christian mourning is not just self-help, and the source of new life is more than merely the process of rediscovering the Christian's own vitalities. Certainly these are engaged, and the process of grieving and mourning is rightly called "work." But Christian mourning is not just "grief work," as commonly described. Rather, it is essentially an experience of divine grace. True, this grace is transmitted largely through human relationships. The beatitude, "Blessed are those who mourn, for they shall be comforted," however, locates the source of comfort in God. We do not just comfort ourselves; we are comforted. It is within this larger view that the process of death and resurrection—to which we now turn—is to be understood as enabling people to do the work of mourning and to grow in a lived experience of the gospel.

C. Steps in the Process

While the events and activities that occur after death do not follow an unfailing pattern, many steps cannot be avoided. Other steps, though optional, like confrontation with the body of the deceased, can be suggested or encouraged. How the various steps are carried out, whether certain steps are included, and what order is followed usually depends significantly on the perceptiveness of the pastor. In order for the process to attend to both death and resurrection, the following fairly typical sequence of steps is recommended:
1. Notification
2. Confrontation
3. Ministries of the supportive community

4. Service of worship
5. The Committal
6. Reentry into the community
7. Continuing support of representatives of the community
8. Recurring memorial acts and services
9. Experience of congregational life.

The event of death has begun the process. If death has been expected, the process may already have partially begun. The removal of an elderly person to a nursing facility, for example, sometimes long before physical death, is often experienced by both the patient and the family as the beginning of death.

1.

Whether death takes place in a hospital, a nursing home, in an accident, or elsewhere, it is usually necessary to notify others. *Notification* sets in motion a series of activities that link together all those for whom the death is significant. These include medical personnel, relatives, perhaps some of the social agencies in the community, neighbors, colleagues. As quickly as possible the pastor, congregation, and funeral director should be notified. The pastor should be notified immediately after the family so that the ministry of suggesting a Christian way through all the decisions that must be made can begin. Indeed, the tone of much of the process, as well as of the funeral service itself, may depend on such early notification. Of course the pastor will not inappropriately interfere nor dictate procedures that offend against expressions of caring and faith most deeply felt by the family. But if the services of a pastor are requested, the duty to help plan the funeral so that it genuinely ministers and witnesses must be discharged. This ministry begins with notification.

Usually the spontaneous reactions of those who witness or learn of death are acts—in some cases ritual acts—of mourning. The traditional covering of the face of the person who has died is one. People may spontaneously rush into each others' arms, cry together, pray, or engage in other expressions that come naturally at such a moment. Often the pastor is present, perhaps having even brought the news. If so, the ability to perceive, to participate, to support, to lead is of great importance. Almost certainly the pastor will offer prayer. However, initiative may rest with someone else, or people may prefer to be alone. Sometimes announcement of a death to a worshiping congregation or other assembly gives rise to spontaneous and powerful emotions that need to be acknowleged, expressed, and perhaps gathered up in prayer or song.

2.

Confrontation of the body of the deceased is important, especially for those whose emotional involvement is great. As a kind of moment of truth, confrontation can be a crossover point when grief begins to move into mourning. Often efforts at denial so dominate emotions and thought that the palpable evidence of death is necessary to move the survivors into reality. This is true for children as well as for adults. Without confrontation with the body, the process of death and resurrection can be disabled at the outset. The bereaved may confront the body at the moment of death, or shortly thereafter when the immediate family wish to see the unprepared body, or at an arranged time for viewing after embalming, or subsequently. In any case, it is important that the occasion and manner of confrontation not be such as to encourage tendencies toward denial. The pastor should be alert to terms and phrases such as: "I'm going to see John," "just the way she was," "asleep," and "slumber," because expressions like these may suggest such a tendency. A genuinely felt admission of the reality of death, insofar as a bereaved person is capable, best fosters spiritual and emotional health.

3.

The *ministries of the supportive community*—family, friends, congregation, community, pastor—are of the greatest importance. Sharing a common sense of loss, the community surrounds the grief-stricken with their physical and spiritual presence. Calling at the house or funeral home, bringing in food, giving assurances of prayer, bringing or sending flowers, sending written messages, assisting with arrangements, are typical forms of ministry. Even when those ministering think they have found nothing to say, each word and gesture bears a certain grace. Because such ministries are exceptions to the routines of life, they mark the intrusion of death and, as such, reinforce its reality. Because they are emotional expressions, they give resonance to grief and provide the climate in which strong feelings can be poured out and healing begins to take place.

Further, when intentionally understood as "ministries," they also mark the members of a congregation as "church." The pastorhood—as well as the priesthood—of believers is made tangible. The Christian graces of faith, hope, and love are visibly acted out. Because the shock of death of one member affects all, the entire congregation can become reengaged with the meanings of death and resurrection. They are turned back on themselves and on their faith. They are recalled as a Christian community to their foundations, made to reexamine their life in Christ, to repent, to renew their faith, and to rededicate themselves to service in Christ's name.

4.

The *service of worship,* commonly spoken of as "the funeral," brings to focus the larger process of death and resurrection. Most of the discussion of this service is reserved for the order and commentary that follow, but selected aspects will be treated here.

First, the funeral service is an act of Christian worship. If it is considered necessary to alter its distinctively Christian character, the service should then not be entitled "A Service of Death and Resurrection." Even though the connection between death and resurrection as defined in biblical faith and as known in common experience be retained, if Christian meanings are not kept sovereign the integrity of the service is lost. Fundamental to any Christian funeral service is the proclamation of Jesus Christ as Savior from death and sin and as Lord of life. Here, as elsewhere in Christian worship, Christ holds the service. He is host; the worshipers are guests. The words and actions of pastor and people are human means through which Christ can save, heal, raise the newness of life; to this healing and salvation, the people respond in the offering of themselves. Thus to name a non-Christian service with a Christian name would be false for all concerned. The pastor should have in mind such essentials as these and realize what is being done if essentials are ignored.

Secondly, the Service of Death and Resurrection is both comforting and confrontational. Or, to speak more accurately, it truly comforts only when it also confronts. Failure to grasp this biblical truth accounts for much of the "corruption" in funeral services today. At stake here is reality—the people's and pastor's sense of reality and the honesty of their intention to be led into reality. Also at stake is the question of what true comfort is. Christian death and resurrection hold implications for faith and morals that cannot be evaded even at such a poignant moment as death. Only as these meanings are made clear will the service honestly deal with what is vital to the people. Otherwise, the existential questions death raises will not be faced; the people will not be ministered to on the deepest levels of their being; and comfort will only be something experienced as emotionally transient on the surface level. Here lies the danger of conceiving the funeral only psychologically and therapeutically. *The Spirit which confronts is the Spirit of truth* as the 14th and 16th chapters of John's Gospel make abundantly clear; and the truth into which the Spirit leads is the evangelical truth of a merciful and moral God, the truth of faith and love, and the truth about ourselves and about life. Not surprisingly, really to be confronted with these meanings does usually become, in one way or another, death and resurrection.

Thirdly, by definition the Christian funeral is corporate. It is an action by a called community that gathers believers as well as all who grieve to whatever degree. Every person is potentially both a mourner and a comforter of others, and all are to do the work of worship together. This corporate character is both visible and invisible. It includes both those physically present and those of all times and places who are gathered in Christ, the communion of saints on earth and in heaven. Consciousness of the communion of saints does not imply, of course, that the reality of death is denied. It does require that the phrase "the living," be given scriptural force and point.

Certain implications flow from this understanding of the service. For one thing, whenever possible the funeral should be conducted in the congregation's regular place of assembly. This very setting reinforces perception of the service as an act of worship. Even when the deceased or family are unconnected with the church, it should not be assumed that a church service is not desired. The act of contacting a minister may itself indicate a reaching out for the ministry and fellowship of the church. The very existence of a church building is a witness to the gospel. Consecrated and dedicated for just such occasions of worship as the Service of Death and Resurrection, it is usually rich in symbols of faith; it evokes memory and association; it is infused with the experience of the worshiping community. It also offers equipment for worship—altar table, hymnals, service books, pulpit Bible, organ, facilities for Holy Communion. If the service is held in a funeral home, everything possible should be done to make the setting proper for Christian worship and to provide symbols of church and faith such as cross, pulpit Bible, vestments, hymnbooks, candles. Above all, the appointments and arrangements should insure that the coffin is not the center of worship.

The gospel, it must be remembered, is experienced and communicated in much more than words. Architecture, stained glass, and the appointments of the church proclaim meaning. Lighted candles also speak of life in the midst of death, summon the believer to watchfulness, and announce the presence of One who is the Light of the world. Flowers symbolize life in the midst of death. Vestments, altar cloths, banners, any special clothing worn by mourners speak of both grief and faith. A cloth pall, designed with Christian symbolism and used to cover the coffin during the service, witnesses to the new life "put on" in Christ. At funerals in some cultures, masks are used. In many Christian traditions, Holy Communion, which engages all our senses, is regularly celebrated. Music variously combines strains of grief and victory. In certain congregations in New Orleans, for example, a marching band plays somber music on the way from the church to the cemetery and exultant jazz music on the return home. Even the way in which pallbearers carry the coffin, the manner in which mourners greet one another, the way in which the pastor welcomes the family to church or funeral home, the bodily movements of people and pastor in processions, the physical conduct of and participation in the service—all such ceremonial and symbol can witness to Christian meanings.

As a corporate act, the service ministers to the congregation as well as to the family. The pastor acts as representative of the congregation and of the universal church. The pastor's personal relationship with the deceased and the family is very important, but pastoral responsibility transcends these relationships. On occasion, for example, a family may request a private service. While sensitive to their feelings, the pastor will strongly discourage this practice. It diminishes the congregational character of worship. It excludes others who by their presence could contribute support to the family. It can close off emotions that need to be expressed. A grief shared is a grief reduced, a grief withheld is a grief amplified. In particular, a private service can deprive mourners of the objective witness of others' faith that can help set the pain felt at death within the promise of experienced renewal.

The corporate nature of the funeral also requires that the congregation participate fully in the service—singing together, praying together, affirming faith together, weeping together. There is no reason why the laity cannot conduct much of the service. The family, also, should be part of the congregation and not isolated from them, and their participation in conducting parts of the service should also be encouraged. Worship, at the Service of Death and Resurrection as elsewhere, belongs to all the people, not to the pastor or the funeral director, or even to the grieving family. Even when no mourners attend and only the pastor and mortuary staff are present, the pastor still represents the church local and universal, visible and invisible, and who can say what pastoral ministry may or may not mean even to the funeral home staff itself at such a time.

5.

The *committal* is usually the next step in the process. However, it is important to observe here that the concept actually has several meanings. First, there is the committal of the physical remains to the earth—or, in the case of cremation, of the body to the elements; this act is provided for in the service of committal in the text below. Secondly, there is the committal of the deceased person to God, and thirdly, the committal—or recommittal—of the people themselves to God. These meanings are interrelated. The latter two, sometimes spoken of liturgically as "commendation" or "offering," are especially evident in the following Service of Death and Resurrection.

Committal in the first meaning of the term may take place immediately following the service of worship or at a later time, depending in part on the place of burial, the distance the body must be transported, cemetery regulations as to when burials may take place, and the season of the year. Committal of the body can also take place immediately after death and be followed by a service of worship in the church, or elsewhere. In any case, whenever possible, the service of committal should be conducted at the burial site. Only when conditions make this unfeasible should it be held in the church, funeral home, or cemetery chapel. Committal of the body or its ashes may be by earth burial, by entombment above ground, by burial at sea, or (in the case of ashes) by scattering. In whatever form, it is to be understood and conducted as an act of worship. For the Christian, the body has been the temple of the Spirit of God. It has been valued and loved. When it no

27

longer serves its purposes in its old form, it is returned to the elements from which it came, with thanksgiving to God for the gift of its wonder. Here the mourners, brought face to face with the finitude of physical life, are thrust back to spiritual realities. For this reason among others, it is desirable that the family be present and participate in this action.

The committal of the deceased person to God is of course implicit throughout the entire process of death and resurrection. Psychologically, many mourners may most poignantly associate it with committal of the remains. Religiously, it comes to fullest expression in various parts of the Service of Death and Resurrection, notably those which name the deceased by name—in the case of a Christian with the "Christian" or baptismal first name, and in intercessory prayer for the dead.

There are strong reasons—historical, theological, liturgical, psychological—in favor of this practice. Protestant aversion to the Roman doctrine of purgatory and reaction against abuses of the mass for the dead have too often become unthinking overreaction and should no longer blind us to the fact that prayer for the dead has been a widespread practice throughout Christian history. It probably derived from Judaism and was an integral part of the Eucharist, which was celebrated in connection with the Christian funeral at least as early as the third century.

Theologically, prayer with the dead is inherent in all Christian worship. Because Christian worship is corporate by definition, the prayer of the church on earth is joined with that of "all the hosts of heaven" who praise and magnify God's holy Name. But Christian prayer is not merely prayer *with*, it is also prayer *for* the dead. As such, it is a profound expression of faith. It is a way of affirming the reality of shared life in Christ's body, a body not subject to temporal and spatial bounds. Even more, prayer for the dead is a profound act of love addressed to a God of love.

The instinct to pray to God for those whom we love and to desire their good is surely as valid for the souls of the departed as for the living. Love—we are rightly told—"*never* fails."

And if love as prayer has been offered for people up until the moment of death, we can hardly expect survivors to cease offering love as prayer after death. Above all, God's love does not cease being the same love after death that it was before, and its very nature is that it is vulnerable to human importunity. Indeed, it is a love whose expression seems to need the human agency of prayer. It is a love, also, that, undeterred by the ignorance of our petitions, translates their meaning in terms of the love behind them. Thus, if one doubts the truth of intercessory prayer for the dead, it would be well to rethink one's understanding of God, one's Christology, and one's doctrine of the church.

Now this does not mean, of course, that such prayer is to be foisted on resistant people. But it does mean that the question of prayer for the dead is a very important one. The pastor may need to reflect on this issue with the congregation as part of their pastoral education without relation to a specific death in their midst.

Committal also takes the form of the offering and reoffering by the people of themselves to God. Liturgically, the offering of the person who has died can be an act through which the people also offer their "very selves," souls and bodies, a living sacrifice holy and acceptable to God, their spiritual service. Thus understood, what is called "the offering of life" in the service becomes the climax of the process of death and resurrection and recapitulates the core reality of Christian faith and experience. Psychologically also, this action is of immense importance. The self in all its brokenness—faith mingled with doubt, love with perhaps bitterness and fear—can be unified in God. Spiritually, the very anguish of offering one's self despite these tangled feelings can be a meeting with Christ in his judgment and mercy, a dying to one's former life and a being raised to a new life. Ethically, committal in this sense can recenter and redirect the self by placing upon it that yoke of love for others by which the self knows that it has passed from death unto life. In short, the offering of self within the contemplation of death acts to illumine the meaning and destiny of life.

Here lies in part the rationale for celebrating Holy Communion in the funeral service. While Communion holds many meanings—thanksgiving, repentance and confession, memorial—its heart is encounter with the crucified and risen Christ, who offers himself to us, and the offering of our life to him.

6.

Reentry into community is usually marked by such actions as the family's last gathering and dispersing, the homely tasks of acknowledging kindnesses and caring for business affairs, resumption of work, and return to the worship and activities of the congregation. One custom in this part of the process calls for special comment—the bringing and sharing of food at what is often a post-service common meal. Not only are practical needs met by this custom; it also exercises much spiritual power. Meals have profound meaning in Christian experience and tradition; it was "in the breaking of bread" that Christ made himself known. The common meal, either in home or church after the committal service, can function as a parallel to Communion. Indeed, the sequence of service of the Word/committal/common meal may be experienced as a unity not unlike the classical pattern of Word and Table. Sensitively understood, this meal can be a means of grace and a source of renewed life. It can do much to restore the mourners to the community around them and symbolize the ongoing nurture which people offer to one another.

7.

The long-range *continuing support* the mourners receive *from representatives of the congregation and community* is vital. In the first days after death has occurred, people usually come in numbers to offer support. However, the time of greatest need usually occurs in the weeks following, when the state of numbing shock has worn off and the sharp reality of loss is experienced, when days are no longer crowded with duties and decisions and there is time to reflect, and when friends and relatives are no longer present to comfort. The pastor's ministry here is vital, but lay people able and willing to enter into a long-range relationship can also be trained to minister at this time and represent to the mourners the larger community. Those who have known grief can be trained to help others deal with grief in its many forms. Questions of faith, of values, of life purpose can be faced together. The ministry of the laity and the priesthood of believers can be made real.

Particularly important are the pastor's first calls on the family after the service and the committal of the body have taken place. The pastor's symbolic and functional roles and the perception of the pastor—as symbol of the gospel and of the church, as friend, as counselor, perhaps as priest—should be rethought here. In these calls the family can be helped to make the transition from initial grief to the long-range work of mourning that lies ahead. The part the pastor can play can be discussed and clarified. Symptoms of normal and abnormal grief can be identified. Estimates can be made of the help that may be necessary in the form of counseling, prayer, rites of penance and absolution, and the administration of Holy Communion. The grieving may also be invited to join, or even help form, a long-term spiritual support group with others of similar needs.

In this part of the process, of course, situations will vary. It must be expected that some people will find more difficulty in experiencing mourning as death and resurrection than others. Some will be better prepared emotionally and spiritually, others less well. Where senility of the deceased or other conditions before death have already caused the relationship with the survivors to be partially or wholly severed, mourning may already be well advanced. Shock will disable others, or personality structure may inhibit or contort. Religious faith may be neurotically or healthily used. The costs of growth in faith and health may be refused and merely temporary adjustment mistaken for resurrection. The pastor must be aware of such possibilities.

8.

From time to time, the mourning process will come to sharper consciousness in *recurring memorial acts and services,* such as Christmas, holidays, birthdays, and anniversaries when the memory of the deceased will be especially poignant; at occasions of other deaths; and when anything else happens that particularly reminds people of death and of those who have died. On such occasions the mourner is particularly open to supportive ministries, such as placing memorial flowers on the grave or in the church, sending handwritten notes of remembrance and sympathy, naming the dead in the church bulletin or service or prayer. Many congregations annually observe the festival of All Saints—on November 1 or on the first Sunday in November—or some other memorial Sunday when the communion of saints is celebrated, and those who have died within the year are named. At weekly Sunday services and especially at the Communion Service, the dead may likewise be remembered in prayer. Through such pastoral and liturgical ministries the meaning of death and resurrection is re-lived; death is faced and life is reaffirmed.

9.

In a broader sense, the mourners' *experience of congregational life* in its totality—through such experiences as its educational program, its evangelism, its mission, and its worship—also conditions the process of death and resurrection. Because the message of death and resurrection is so central in Scripture and in the church's faith, it should inform the total life of the congregation. The way people deal with death when it comes will depend on how forceful the impact of this message has been upon their consciousness through the structures of congregational life. Death and life after death are commonly perceived in our culture today, for example, in secular and pseudoscientific terms; and lay people's attitudes are more often shaped by newspaper journalism, magazines, films, and paperback best sellers than by Christian teaching. Certainly, changing attitudes toward death and the supernatural are to be learned from, and death and resurrection identified in our experience generally. The discerning pastor, however, will take care that a congregation's educational program helps people to know the Christian meaning of these realities, and to distinguish truth from fad, faith from superstition, and Christian teaching from occult speculation.

Similarly, congregational evangelism needs to be scrutinized in light of the death-resurrection message. Evangelism in some congregations today appears to result in a programmed experience of easy grace rather than a costly dying and rising with Christ. But only as a fatefulness of a decision for Christ is brought home to people in a congregation's evangelistic outreach can they deal as Christians with fate, death, and resurrection outside the context of that decision.

Mission, likewise, requires a congregation to be aware of the forces of death and evil in society—such as militarism, racism, greed, sexism, corruption, hedonism, materialism, oppression—and to affirm life over against them. Truly, death and the diabolic bear many faces; physical death is only one of them. Likewise resurrection as God's calling into being of not-yet-existent-life takes many forms, and in a profound sense the mission of a congregation is precisely to be agents of resurrection amidst forces of social death. To pass from death into life is not an experience reserved until people die physically. Christians can know this experience now.

Probably the ongoing worship life of a congregation most powerfully determines people's perception of death and resurrection at the funeral as well as in the process that encompasses it. Insofar as preaching, the Lord's Supper, baptism, confirmation, and other renewals of the baptismal covenant have been structured by this central message, it will be real; insofar as they have not, it will not be real. Indeed, only as the total spectrum of congregational worship is formed by the theme of death and resurrection can it vitally form people in Christian faith. This is why the frame of the Christian year is so crucial. Its very pivot is the Christian Passover of Maundy Thursday/Good Friday/Easter. Its seasons and festivals are but variations on this theme, and in its totality it is the drama of Christian reality within which all else unfolds. Thus a kind of judgment on a congregation's worship life is pronounced at its funerals. Whether people come to times of bereavement poorly or well prepared says much about the integrity of congregational worship as the people have experienced it.

D. Memorial Services

Many persons have requested resources for *memorial services* and for use in the event that the body is cremated or donated for medical purposes. The term "memorial service" denotes a service at which the body is not present, as distinct from a funeral where the coffin containing the remains is at hand. Often the question is raised whether the memorial pattern is fundamentally different from the funeral and calls for a different kind of service.

In dealing with this issue, it is important to emphasize that every funeral in one sense is a memorial service. Further, it is important to distinguish several different types of services frequently called memorial services.

(1) There are annual memorial services *commemorating the dead,* such as those mentioned above. Many congregations hold such services, as do many secular groups, such as veterans' organizations. These are highly appropriate as part of the process of experiencing death and resurrection, as preparation for the death of participants, and as a continuation of the work of mourning for those who grieve.

(2) Memorial services are also held *on the anniversary of the birth or death* of prominent historical figures such as Abraham Lincoln or Martin Luther King. Jewish Yahrzeit rites on the anniversary of the death of a member of one's family are an example from another religious tradition.

(3) Sometimes memorial services are held *in addition to a funeral service* for the benefit of those unable to attend the funeral. Mourners may live too far from the scene of the funeral to attend. The time or the season of the year may not be convenient. Those who wish to attend may be hospitalized or otherwise incapacitated, and a simple memorial service in

the hospital or home may be appropriate. When a very well-known person dies, the family may wish a less public funeral followed by a larger memorial service.

(4) A memorial service is sometimes held *in place of a funeral.* Probably this is the type of service most commonly referred to when the question of memorial services is raised. Such a service is sometimes held because the body of the deceased has been destroyed or cannot be recovered or for some other reason is unavailable. The body may have been donated for medical purposes or buried without public ceremony by family decision or out of respect for the expressed wishes of the person who has died. A similar situation arises with cremation, the reduction of the body to ashes by fire. Sometimes the body is cremated without the mourners' having the opportunity to confront it, sometimes following such a confrontation but before a public service, sometimes following the public service. The ashes may be buried in the ground, placed in a vault above ground, or scattered.

Such a variety of possibilities makes clear the wisdom of being cautious in making blanket generalizations about memorial services. A few general observations, however, can be made.

Most orders of service for funeral or burial, including the Service of Death and Resurrection that follows, can be adapted for a memorial service and for use at a cremation or a body donation; indeed, a memorial service should generally contain as far as possible the same elements as a funeral. The committal of the body will, of course, be eliminated. If the pastor has been asked to serve in the office of Christian minister and the family and mourners consider the occasion to be Christian worship, the Christian gospel should certainly be proclaimed at a memorial service as at other services of the church. Perhaps the service may focus more directly on the life of the deceased than at the funeral; but this change should not be too difficult, and the integrity of the service as a Christian service need not be impaired. In fact, the following service provides for this change in the optional acts of "naming" and

35

"witness" (as explained in the Commentary) more aptly than traditional funeral services have. Prayers, lessons, music given in Additional Resources also take into account a wide range of situations and can readily be adapted to various circumstances.

As already mentioned, the service with the body present is to be preferred, however. This practice is in accord with Jewish-Christian tradition and its respect for the body as part of human and Christian being. It also accords with an instinct deep in our nature: the desire to affirm the person of the deceased by honoring the body, really, the instinct to love. It is not exaggeration to say that the presence of the body marks the incarnational nature of human love, and a service without such a visible reminder in a sense denatures love of that which most poignantly conveys its reality. The presence of the body can also protect against the tendency to spiritualize death away and to gloss over its starkness. New Testament faith does not shrink from such confrontation—death is death. Further, such confrontation therapeutically contributes to making the mourning process less difficult. For the living, resurrection depends on internalizing the reality of death. Only as this internalization is painfully lived through and appropriated can full healing usually take place. Psychiatric evidence of the ill effects when internalization does not take place underscores this point.

At services where the body is not present, it is important to do what is possible to facilitate the confrontation with and realization of death. The language used should not evade reality. Visible reminders such as pictures or other tokens of the person who has died can also help. It may be possible to provide the opportunity prior to the services for those who wish to see the body to do so, especially the immediate family. At the final disposition of the remains, by whatever method, care should be taken straightforwardly to name death as death, and body as body.

THE MINISTRY OF THE CHURCH AT DEATH

E. *For Those Outside the Church*

Another question frequently arises. What kind of service should be held for *non-Christians or the unchurched?* Frequently, services are requested for people who have formally belonged to the Christian community but have given no evidence of Christian commitment, who have not been church members though they have considered themselves Christian, who have professed a religion other than Christianity, or who have professed no religion at all. Furthermore, whatever the religious commitment of the deceased, there may be the widest differences of religious commitment among the mourners. The suggestion has been made that a special service or services be provided for such occasions.

After careful consideration, it has seemed best not to do so in this book. A variety of worship materials and resources is provided with this service which can be adapted to diverse situations. The Christian pastor is free to minister as may be judged appropriate according to circumstances. Certainly it is important always to be circumspect in concluding how any person stands before God. Further, and common to all people—Christian or non-Christian, churched or un-churched—is the basic respect for every human life and, correspondingly, the instinct to provide a decent burial. Surely the pastor's duty and desire will be to honor this respect. The Service of Death and Resurrection is not to be an occasion for rejection or manipulation but for genuine caring and outreach.

At the same time, a Service of Death and Resurrection is intended to be a proclamation of the gospel, but there should be no conflict between this affirmation and the requirements of sensitive pastoral care. There is every reason to assume that when people request the services of a Christian minister, whatever their religious commitment, they expect the minister to minister as a Christian; and surely the minister's own conduct and sensitivity can be a Christian witness. The gospel here may be better acted than spoken, but it can also be spoken in ways that respect the integrity of the hearers. The

37

minister's witness need be no less a proclamation of the gospel if, out of respect for others, the service is not held in the church building or is not called a Service of Death and Resurrection or omits certain lessons, prayers, or creeds that might give offense. If circumstances call for sharing leadership of a service with someone of a different religious commitment, surely each can witness with integrity while respecting the faith of the other.

Indeed, there is probably ambivalence in all who mourn, which should be faced openly in the perspective of the gospel. Each of us brings to death and grief a mixture of doubt and faith, of fear and confidence, of that which makes for death and that which makes for life. It is precisely in the light and strength of the gospel that we can look honestly at all this, be humbled before truth, enter more fully into reality about ourselves and God, and find help in time of need.

In this vein we also address what must be for some ministers the hardest question: how can I help others and give them the assurance they need if my own faith is faltering? One may find an answer in Paul's insight. We are "stewards of the mysteries of God" (I Corinthians 4:1). We are servants and agents of a grace whose efficacy does not depend on our own faith or virtue. As stewards do not possess what is entrusted to them, so ministers who read the great passages of Scripture, pray the prayers of the church, preach a gospel they themselves do not entirely understand, and allow Christian symbols to be seen and music of faith heard are letting God make them instruments of a gospel greater than the feeble faith any of us can bring. The minister can surely receive as well as give at the Service of Death and Resurrection.

F. The Ministries of Others

The officiating minister should be sensitive to the ministries performed by others. Many are called upon to minister at the time of death, and the pastor's ability or inability to work with them can greatly help or hinder the effectiveness of these ministries.

For the benefit of all concerned, the pastor should have a sound working relationship with the funeral directors of the community. In hardly any other public capacity does the pastor work so closely with another care-taking profession. Rivalry or misunderstandings can disserve the bereaved and interfere with a properly conducted funeral. It is wise, as early as possible in a pastorate, for the pastor to make friends with the funeral directors in the community and discuss with them how all can best cooperate. The pastor's perception of the nature of the funerals and of its proper conduct should be made clear, as should the perceptions and policies of the funeral director. Differences and disagreements should be worked out in a spirit of mutual understanding and respect.

Good relationships between pastor and church and funeral-home musician are also important. It is vital that the musician respect the pastor's role and authority as the leader of worship and as the one having a unique relationship with the mourners. It is also vital that the pastor respect the musician's standards and musical integrity. Both should discuss in advance their views on such questions as the qualities that make music suitable for worship at a funeral and the place of congregational singing, of solos, of live instrumental music, and of recorded music. How does one determine, for example, when a solo is a helpful witness, a true act of worship, an artistic display, or a too-easy substitute for congregational participation? Prior to a service the pastor should be consulted by musician and family regarding the purpose and place of music in the service. Rather than attempting to serve as intermediary between family and musician, however, the wise pastor will refer the family to the musician.

Similarly, the pastor needs to understand the ways in which friends and family minister to one another. Customs and practices which may at first sight seem strange often have in them much wisdom when the total context is known. There are rich varieties of ethnic practices, many regional folk customs, and wide diversity in the traditions of particular families and in individual expectations. These are not without fault of course, but given the background out of which they come they often make excellent sense. Two people may be mourning with equal honesty; one may cry profusely, even scream, while the other weeps inconspicuously and silently. Music that comforts some people will seem inappropriate to others. Some people perceive distinctive styles of clothing as appropriate for funerals, while to others the question does not matter. An elaborate floral display, a single rosebud, or a donation to a significant cause may each be, from their respective donors, the most eloquent of gifts. A magnificent casket that some people would consider a terrible waste of money, a simple casket that others might consider stingy, a pall covering a casket of whatever sort, may each, in context, be true expressions of faith and caring. The value of a funeral is determined not by its financial cost nor by its conformity to a particular custom, but by the effectiveness of its Christian witness and of its ministry to people.

Understanding and sensitivity are especially needed between people of different generations. Mourners at the death of persons in their teens or twenties, for instance, will include parents and others of the parents' and grandparents' generations as well as friends of the deceased and, perhaps, brothers and sisters and their spouses of more or less the same age. What seems loving and appropriate to one group of mourners may not seem so to another. When the untimeliness of a death and perhaps its violent nature as well—by accident or suicide, or as a result of crime or war—have caused grief to be exceptionally intense, one group of mourners may especially need to be made more sensitive to the emotions and needs of another.

G. Children and Death

It is also important to be sensitive to the impact of death upon children. A child can have a vital, full emotional life, and religious faith, although framed by limited experience. Children can know acute grief even though they do not understand the meaning of death. They, too, need opportunity for ceremonial acting out in order to grow in faith and to deal with their feelings. Sometimes adults—perhaps projecting their own anxieties—determine that children should not attend a funeral. Studies have shown, however, that children are more likely to be emotionally injured by being denied the opportunity to confront the body of a dead person and to experience a funeral service than by being allowed to participate at their own level of understanding. Just as a flower girl does not need to understand all about marriage and human sexuality in order to perform her role at a wedding, so a child does not need to understand all about death in order to participate in a funeral. This is why the following service provides for the participation of children.

We need always to remember that children are threatened by deceit. Deceit not only denies them the answers they require for healthful growth in understanding, it also undermines confidence in those to whom they look for understanding. Children have built-in sensitivities to lies. They perceive when they have been denied the truth, and distrust may impel them to use their imaginations in damaging ways. While it is unwise to force a child to attend a funeral, a child's refusal to share in such an important family activity may signal that already a child is responding to anxiety in a damaging way. Children need direct, honest, and simple answers to their questions. Either to deny an answer or to over-answer is to foster anxiety in a child's life.

Adults should also be aware of the developmental process and of the stages of a child's capacity for awareness and for perception, and should respond to children's needs according to their level. Children have long lives ahead of them, and it is extremely important that they be guided into healthful attitudes toward death and into honest faith. Mishandled anxiety in the face of death—and the unhealthy fantasy it fosters—has been shown to be one cause of nonrational behaviour, indulging in drugs, and playing life-threatening games. A realistic confrontation that includes even a certain fear of death, on the other hand, when set within supportive relationships and religious faith, can stabilize behavior and enable a child to cope with other fears that life inevitably brings. From the funeral experience, children can learn that their own life is valued and valuable, and that it is in the hands of a loving God.

H. Conclusion

The purpose of this interpretation of the Service of Death and Resurrection, and the larger process of which it is a part, is to restate the Christian gospel in its integrity for the church's pastoral and liturgical ministry today. Undoubtedly, the thought in this effort will be felt by some readers to reflect certain insensitivities and an all too limited understanding. The authors themselves are quite aware that much more can be said. Yet, they hope it may be a way station toward more committed and competent ministry in the years to come, and in this spirit the authors invite criticisms and suggestions.

II. Commentary on the Service

A. Gathering of the People

A Liturgical Perspective

An order of service should provide for proclaiming the gospel in a way that authentically ministers to people. This proclamation is initiated in the gathering. Proclaiming (from *clamo,* meaning "to call" or "cry aloud") is first of all, however, an action of God that precedes, although it also takes form in, the people's action. Gathering is thus the people acting out the nature of Christian assembly as both divine convocation (from *con vocare* meaning "to call together") and human congregation (from *con grex* meaning "together," "flock"). It is the people defining themselves as "the called," that is, as the ecclesia (from the Greek *ek kaleo* meaning "call out"), in short, as church. The first emphasis, however, is upon God and upon the priority of his grace in calling and recalling through Jesus Christ. In bodily movement, gesture, music, spoken words, and symbols, pastor and people simultaneously express and are impressed with this meaning.

However, assembly at the Christian funeral is distinctive because of the extent to which it literally takes place in the face of death. Mercy and judgment and the promise of resurrection are inseparable realities of the gospel. To some degree, the funeral gathering, like other gatherings of the church, should be a time of critical confrontation with those realities, with that gospel. This does not mean that either the gathering or the funeral is to be threatening or predominantly penitential. Nor is the seriousness of the occasion to be equated with somberness. Joy contrapuntally mingles with sorrow. What the confrontation does mean is that the funeral is in part a "converting" and a "reconverting" ordinance; hence, the gathering begins both a salvational and a healing event. In this sense the funeral is a liturgical microcosm of the arresting truth: "You he made alive while you were dead in trespasses and sins" (see Ephesians 2:1-10). The people will perceive this meaning unevenly. It may become real only as the service progresses or at a later time, or it may not become real at all. Yet, the funeral can truthfully be an "Easter Liturgy," as it is often described, only if it is also in some sense a "Good Friday Liturgy." In Christian experience the "Hallelujah Chorus" and the "Lord, Have Mercy" go together. The gathering initiates this realization.

Probably the pastor will open the gathering and lead the liturgy. The service, however, is not the pastor's but the church's and the people's (this is the truth underlying the principles of corporateness and participation noted in the previous chapter). The liturgical requirement in the gathering is not only that the people become physically present. Even more, they act to manifest their presence to one another before God so that a communion is established in which they can do the work of worship together. Therefore, throughout the gathering the people should be fully involved although naturally and without manipulation. For this reason, among others, the order of service should be available for use by the congregation.

[*Welcome, Coffin Processional*]

Too often the gravity of the funeral service becomes a disabling stiffness. A certain solemnity is almost inevitable, but there is no reason why pastor, friends, and members of the congregation should not welcome the family and other mourners to the place of the service in a natural way. Perhaps in a room other than the sanctuary, greetings may be exchanged, prayer offered, music sung, food shared, letters and messages read, pictures and objects associated with the deceased displayed and talked about. Local custom will no doubt affect decisions here, but the point is that the human character of the congregation should find natural, unaffected expression. This human touch may occur in other parts of the service or at an occasion after the service.

In preparation for the service, candles in the chancel may

be lit. The coffin, if not already in place, may be covered with a pall, perhaps in the vestibule or narthex. Music may be offered, a procession formed.

Generally, it is desirable to cover the coffin with a pall, as illustrated.

Palls, or patterns from which church members can make a pall, are readily available from church supply houses; or members of a congregation may design and make their own. A pall denotes the community and democracy of all members. More importantly, it connects the service with the new life a Christian puts on at Baptism and prefigures the purification of soul that faith looks forward to in Christ. The family or friends of the deceased may place the pall over the coffin. As they do so, the pastor may say the words printed in brackets immediately after the greeting; "Christ has died. . . ." If so used, these sentences are omitted after the greeting. The pall may be removed after the recessional or when the coffin is placed in the hearse.

The liturgical color used in the service for the pall, the pastor's stole, and the chancel paraments should signify the meanings of the gospel of death and resurrection. Green or white is appropriate. Green signifies new life and growth. White signifies both death and resurrection. White is widely used as a color of mourning in many African and Asian cultures, and even in Western cultures an association of the color white with death is shown, for instance, in the phrase "white as a ghost." In Christian tradition and practice, however, white has been predominantly used to symbolize the triumph of Easter, new life, purity, joy, and celebration.

The power of a procession to ritualize meaning should not be underestimated. It acts out the coming in and the coming together of the assembly. As a rite of passage and upholding, it focuses the meanings that the larger process of death and resurrection holds for the grieving. Especially, it gives physical form to the aspiration of the people's souls toward God. It may be elaborate or simple; indeed, its very simplicity can witness powerfully. Rigid positioning need not govern its order. Usually, however, the minister(s), choir, pallbearers carrying the coffin, the bereaved (if they have not previously been seated), and perhaps official representatives from associations to which the deceased belonged, follow in succession. Children, grandchildren, or other family members may carry flowers, the family Bible, or symbols of the life and work of the deceased. A member of the congregation may precede or follow the clergy carrying the pulpit Bible; deacons or others may bear the paschal (Easter) or other candle and bread and wine for the Lord's Supper if it is to be celebrated; if a cross is to be brought in, the bearer of it heads the procession. In both processional and recessional, the coffin should be physically carried by the pallbearers as a sign of respect, rather than being rolled in on wheels.

The seating of the participants should be explained to them in advance, and provision should also be made for placing of the cross, Communion elements, candle, and Bible if there are such. Lighted candles on stands may also be placed around the coffin, perhaps at the corners. Agreement should also be made with pallbearers and the funeral director to position the coffin at right angles to the altar table, not laterally, with the head of the coffin nearest the altar table. If Communion is to be administered, however, the coffin may need to be located differently, depending on the architecture and chancel appointments, so that access to the Communion rail, or to appropriate stations for serving the people is provided. The coffin should remain closed during the service and, except in unusual circumstances, thereafter as well.

[The Word of Grace]

If a hymn is not sung or music offered during the procession, the pastor opens the service by saying the Word of grace as he precedes the coffin in the procession; the people are standing. If the coffin is in place and there is no procession, the Word of grace is spoken from the chancel, the people standing. The pastor may choose to speak the opening word from a lower elevation, perhaps near the head of the coffin and nearer to the people.

The phrase the "Word of grace" is used intentionally to convey several meanings simultaneously. "Word" means God's self-disclosure and self-giving. "Grace" suggests the active reality of God's love in calling, meeting, and dealing with the people. The printed text—taken from John's Gospel and the book of Revelation—is obviously Christ-centered, just as grace is. Through the text, Christ's voice opens the service; its words are sayings attributed by the faithful to Christ himself. His mysterious presence is offered. The cosmic meaning of his victory over death and evil is declared. His life is promised now and in the future.

Alternative sentences for the Word of grace are found in Resources.

[Greeting]

The greeting states the purpose of the service as praise and proclamation. Within this frame, it also marks in a natural way the human character of the assembly. It realistically recognizes the emotions of the people—grief, loss, pain—and personalizes the service without making it too personal by naming the deceased (see also the commentary on "naming" and "witness").

The optional biblical sentences after the greeting, beginning "Christ has died . . . ," culminating in the promise of I John 3:2-3, set the human life of the deceased within the divine life of Christ first "put on" as a child of God born at Baptism. At the same time, they quietly affirm the hope of life with Christ after death for all people of faith.

While saying these words the pastor may turn and directly face or take up a position near the coffin, perhaps extending an arm over it at the sentence: "As in Baptism . . . " However, the sentences beginning "Here and now . . ." should be spoken directly to the people.

[Hymn or Song]

The term "song" is introduced in the gathering and appears throughout this service. The term is biblical; it is meant to suggest that in general, vocal music is preferable to instrumental; it is less restrictive in meaning than "hymn," although it certainly includes hymns, and it is especially intended to enlist the participation of the people.

The location of song in the opening of the service is at the discretion of the pastor. It may come before, during, or after the processional, or after the Word of grace, the greeting [and sentences]. A strong congregational hymn on the greatness and goodness of God is most appropriate here.

[Suggested Guidelines for Music]

1. Music is faith and doctrine experienced in one of their most powerful forms. Great care should be taken with it. Music at the funeral is not to be used as psychological manipulation or soothing syrup. It is to proclaim the gospel and provide for the people's response.
2. Music is servant of the liturgy and should be liturgically evaluated.
3. Because the service is a congregational act and declares the church's faith, its quality as church music must therefore be set beside other considerations, including the wishes of the family. Actually, tension between these need not arise, given sensitive guidance by pastor and musician. In the church's faith the individual's faith is expressed and strengthened.
4. Familiar music is usually best, although on occasion music

of Christian integrity and strength—like the gospel itself—may seem to be "over against" the people as well as "for" them. Interpretation and education in liturgical music should have been undertaken long before the funeral in the life of the congregation.

5. Music should be chosen in consultation with the organist or music leader. A current list of appropriate selections is available from the Section on Worship, PO Box 840, Nashville, Tennessee 37202.

6. If the congregation is not large enough to enable congregational singing, a song may be played on an instrument or sung as a solo or by a choir. Generally, singing by the congregation is preferred.

7. If live music is not possible and only recorded music is available, music of Christian faith and of strength, well performed, should be selected.

8. Music may be chosen from any period, ancient to contemporary.

9. Texts in keeping with the Christian view of death and resurrection should be chosen.

10. Music selected should be performed in a manner that exemplifies the Christian stance on death and resurrection, so that the Easter faith is expressed.

[Prayer]

The nature of prayer at this point will be determined partly by the kinds of prayer offered elsewhere in the service. An overview of all the elements of prayer should be kept in mind. However, petition for God's help, thanksgiving for the communion of saints, confession of sin and assurance of pardon seem especially fitting here although other kinds of prayer may certainly be offered. Other prayers than those printed in the text may of course be used; these only illustrate types of prayer that seem fitting. In form, a pastoral prayer here is appropriate, or a series of prayers, perhaps collects, from the Resources or other materials, or a carefully prepared litany. See the guidelines below.

The option of the traditional responses—said or sung—is

provided: "The Lord be with you"; "And also with you." These both invite and affirm the Lord's presence. They also anticipate the prayer that follows as response to the already present Lord, and even as, in a sense, inspired by him. They mutually involve pastor and people in a corporate way. They are part of ancient tradition. Their use here is consonant with their use in other services and is recommended.

Prayer for God's help is placed first in this service because it fits the situation of the people and marks the primal reality of all Christian prayer: human finitude and dependence upon God, God's vulnerability to our dependence, and God's grace answering to our human need. The Christian consciousness of God is basically defined by the belief that ultimately God is affected by the human cry of need, that God possesses not merely intelligence and will but also pathos. The content of the petition invokes biblical meanings such as grace, light, life, love, and thrusts to the heart of the gospel in the great Pauline paradox of death and life in Romans 8 and 14.

The second prayer of thanksgiving and intercession for the communion of saints contrasts human mortality with God's eternity. Even more it is prayer of the Christian community embracing those who pray on earth with those in the church above. Devotion concentrically moves from "saints" understood as "all," through those "dear to us," to "your child *(name)*." The petitions for peace and light perpetual are widespread in the funeral liturgies of Christendom. The "home not made with hands," while originally referring to the celestial "body" the Christian puts on at the consummation of all things, is an apt metaphor for marking the sense of final destiny, the homecoming faith looks forward to.

The prayer of confession conveys the Christian vision of moral reality, the kindness and the severity of God that judges, heals, and saves. This prayer is rightly purgative and is meant to deal with the sense of failure, fear, and guilt that grief often brings. However, it is also salvational. Before the holy God, sin is named in some of its elemental forms. These constitute a kind of death from which God's love can deliver into life.

Any or all of these prayers may be used, and each can be introduced with an appropriate bidding sentence perhaps followed by a response. Such acts successively regrasp the people's consciousness and redirect their devotion. Before the petition, the pastor may say: "Blessed be God by whose great mercy we have been born anew to a living hope through the Resurrection of Jesus Christ. In his Name let us pray"; and the people respond, "Hear us, Lord." Before the thanksgiving: "Let us thank God for all the faithful dead, and pray for *(name)*"; and the people respond, "Into your mercy, Lord, receive *(name's)* soul." Before the confession: "Let us confess our sins unto God": the people, "O Lamb of God, who takes away the sins of the world, have mercy upon us." The Kyrie ("Lord, have mercy upon us. Christ, have mercy . . . Lord, have mercy . . .") is appropriate here as elsewhere in the service (see *The Book of Hymns* 834, 838, and 839).

[Pardon]

The assurance of pardon is essential. Without it, the gospel as redemption and healing, as death and resurrection, is incompletely proclaimed. While the words of pardon may at times seem rhetorical, actually the pastor is here agent of a grace able to do abundantly more than we can know or think. Further, the pastor has been called to this function just as all Christians have been called to be priests to one another. Only so can ministry be mutually fulfilled and the church as Christ's Body be purified and built up. The words of absolution used here consist of St. Paul's sentences in Romans 8:34 and I Corinthians 15:57, and reference again is to the fugal theme of death and resurrection (other versions are found in Resources).

[Suggested Guidelines for the Prayers]

1. The whole service in a sense is a prayer and should be conducted accordingly. As its name signifies, *A Service of Death and Resurrection* deals with the central truth of the gospel and the deepest drama in the soul's religious experience. Significantly, Scripture and tradition speak of

this as the "saving mystery." The language and form of the prayers should aim to be worthy of this reality.

2. For most people, prayer is the heart of worship. For others, music may be the central feature, although much if not most of liturgical music is also prayer. Nothing so deeply meets people's needs at the funeral or so authentically heals. Indeed, *the funeral service is best thought of as prayer-centered* rather than sermon-centered.

3. All the prayers, and all of any single prayer, should be addressed to God (or Christ or the Holy Spirit). The focus and the thrust are toward Divine Reality at the same time that the prayers grasp and lift up the human condition. Thus, speech about God in the third person is to be avoided. Prayer should address God in the second person as "you" or "thou."

4. Usually, all the essential elements of prayer—praise, thanksgiving, confession and absolution, petition, intercession, offering or dedication, commendation, ascription, acclamation—will find place in greater or lesser degree in the funeral, in songs, lessons, and elsewhere, in addition to the prayers. Some of the elements will be explicit, some implicit. However, the elements of thanksgiving and offering of life are especially to be stressed.

5. The prayers may be spontaneously offered or prayed from a full text or notes. In any case they should be prepared in the pastor's mind and soul, freshly for each occasion.

6. While the pastor will usually prepare and offer the prayers, they are not to be just the pastor's self-expression. Rather, they are to express the church's faith. The pastor represents the whole church and prays as its servant and in its name.

7. Prayers at the service may be original with the pastor and prepared for the occasion, or taken from the church's heritage of prayer, or express the local or ethnic heritage of the congregation; or they may combine these.

8. Some styles of praying are so essentially oral, rather than literary, that they are better transmitted by hearing and remembering than by reading from the printed page. The selection of printed prayers in this book cannot include examples of such styles, but they have vital place and importance in the church's worship.

9. Care should be taken in altering the archaic language of traditional prayers not to do violence to their cadence, phrasing, and rhythm.

10. The forms of prayer can vary. The pastoral prayer is one form. A coherent sequence of short sections of prayer is another; these may be prefaced with words of bidding and guidance, such as, "Let us offer God our thanksgiving for his church, the communion of saints." Several collects may be grouped together. There may be a litany in which the people participate responsively. Spontaneous prayers, or concerns to be gathered up in prayer, may be invited from the congregation.

11. While the manner and mood of prayers at the service are usually solemn, the leader should take care that they are not voiced in an intentionally morbid fashion.

12. Prayers should be true to the experience of the people, faithful to Christian doctrine, simple and unaffected. Liturgical taste and style vary, but the following values should be kept in mind: a sense of the holy, simplicity, clarity, force, movement rhythm, cadence, beauty, location of emphasis, sound, word color, image, evocative power, and psychological association.

[Psalm]

The use of Psalm 130 here and of Psalm 23 later in the service is to be distinguished from the use of the psalms provided as lections that follow shortly in the proclamation. Psalm 130, whether said or sung, functions here as a canticle or song. In its total meaning it voices the situation of the people before God and recapitulates the drama of death and resurrection and marks the salvational character of the service. It expresses mercy and judgment, trust and fear, forgiveness and guilt, the future and the present, and as such combines both redemption and healing. Functionally, it draws together and concludes the gathering, and provides a moment of liturgical rest before the people turn to the work of proclamation. Ever since John Wesley heard it sung on the day of his Aldersgate experience, Psalm 130 has been prominent in Wesleyan tradition.

The version given here is taken, with modifications, from the King James Bible because of its intrinsic power and beauty. Other versions, as well as other psalms, could be used.

At a funeral or memorial service for non-Christians or unchurched persons, this psalm may not be appropriate, and could be omitted altogether or replaced by another psalm.

B. Proclamation and Praise

A Liturgical Perspective

The entire Service of Death and Resurrection in one sense is proclamation. As with all Christian worship, the test both of the whole and of the parts is whether the service is kerygmatic—that is, whether the gospel is proclaimed in a way that ministers to people. Of course, no single service and no single part can adequately do this, but surely the funeral must embody the gospel as fully and faithfully as possible. At the same time, a funeral is no place for the peripheral or trivial or merely sentimental, and the fatefulness of the experience of death must be matched with the fatefulness of the gospel. In this section, proclamation is forthrightly named and centered in Scripture and sermon.

The arrangement of Scriptures follows the traditional sequence in Christian worship of Old Testament, Epistle (or New Testament lection other than from the Four Gospels), and reading from the Gospels. Readings should not be a hodgepodge; rather, they should be selected to embody the integrity and fullness of the gospel, and culminate in words attributed to Jesus himself in the Gospels. This principle governs the choice of "preferred" and "recommended" lections and gives them unity, sequence, and dramatic movement.

Isaiah 40 (or alternatively Isaiah 43, 55, or the Passover-Exodus narrative, such as Exodus 14) strongly proclaims the Old Testament meanings of death and resurrection. Certain "recommended" psalms also do this, although psalms normally serve more as acts of praise. If used as lections, their function should be understood as different from the use of Psalm 23 as a gradual (transition) between Old and New Testament readings, and from Psalm 130 used earlier as a canticle.

In the New Testament, I Corinthians 15 forthrightly proclaims the theme of death and resurrection with reason and passion: "First and foremost, I handed on to you the facts . . . that Christ died . . . was buried . . . was raised . . . and appeared . . . " (vv. 3-5, NEB). Here death and resurrection are unequivocally declared as historical event, and then interpreted. Thus this Epistle appropriately precedes the poetry of such readings as Revelation 21 and 22 ("the new heaven," "the new earth," "the holy city"), and the readings culminate in the great assurance of John's Gospel: "Let not your hearts be troubled . . . I am the way . . . Because I live, you will live also" (14:1, 6, 19). Alternatively, selections from Romans 8, II Corinthians 4, Ephesians 1, I Peter 1, Revelation 7, and especially the Emmaus narrative in Luke 24 manifest death and resurrection.

The sermon, though brief, should primarily be a proclamation of Christ and his gospel, not an eulogy nor an impressionistic meditation, not a moral or theological lecture, nor manufactured inspiration or psychological therapy. However, while proclamatory, the sermon is not a one-way thunderbolt. It is to be verified by its ministering quality. It is human speech through which Christ the Word tenderly, truthfully, healingly engages the souls of the people where they are in their hurt and need. It is a means of verbal grace potentially as sacramental and sacrificial as the bread and wine of Communion—that God's Spirit may use to raise people into newness of life. And it anticipates the people's response in the offering of their lives that follows.

While the sermon should not be primarily eulogy, the particular death and grief of the occasion needs to be recognized in its human character. The sermon should not be so depersonalized that reference to the deceased and the mourners is eliminated. If some funerals are too personalized, others are too impersonal. The pastor will need to walk a liturgical fine line here as well as throughout the service. The optional acts of naming and witness may be of help. In any case, each sermon should be sensitively and freshly prepared for the particular occasion. While the pastor does the preparing, however, it is the Lord's Word and the church's faith that speak.

[Scripture Lections, Psalm, Sermon]

Readings from Christian Scripture are essential in all funeral services conducted by a Christian minister; it is hard to think of a situation where this would not be the case. If nonscriptural readings are used, they should supplement, not displace, Scripture. Great care should be exercised in deciding to use them and in selecting them. Their liturgical quality should be evaluated alongside Scripture; often the very contrast will decide the matter. Their appropriateness as expressions of the church's faith needs to be weighed against personal preference, emotional attachment, popularity.

Particular situations may require particular readings appropriate to them. The Resources list readings for the funerals of children or youth, for the non-Christian and unchurched, for an untimely or tragic death. Closer scrutiny, however, may reveal that the customary lections fit the situation better than may first have been supposed.

Lections may be chosen from any Bible version of integrity and good liturgical quality. Various versions should be consulted and compared. When passages are elided or condensed, essential meaning should be preserved. Punctuation may be changed, although not irresponsibly, to facilitate flow of meaning. Occasionally, different translations using both ancient and modern forms may be fused together if this serves liturgical purpose. The clarity characteristic of modern translations is always important, but in good liturgy, translational accuracy is not the maximum value. Certain verbal usages in more traditional versions, while not as "modern" as we might wish, often have a landmark quality to them that can hardly be changed without impoverishment.

The place, means, manner, and posture of reading and hearing are important. These symbolically convey—or fail to convey—vital meanings that are really an acted-out commentary on the gospel. They are not just "ritualism"; in their way, they too proclaim. A prayer for illumination, for example, asking the Spirit's guidance in hearing and understanding God's Word, not only can provide a transition from the preceding psalm, but also signals that human speaking and hearing are at the service of a Reality greater and other than the reader or preacher, and mark the people's duty—as well as the pastor's—both to hear and speak the Word. However, this prayer may also be dispensed with, as the very gravity of the funeral occasion itself communicates a sense of waiting upon God. Also, prayer is abundantly provided for elsewhere.

Customarily, lections are read from pulpit or lectern. They may also be read near or from the midst of the people, especially the climactic reading from the Gospels. Such an action signifies that proclamation is not only to the congregation; it also rises from and centers in the congregation. The people may be asked to stand for the reading from the Gospel. This posture, practiced in the church from at least the fourth century, summons and concentrates the people's attention by signaling the sacredness and uniqueness that attach to words attributed to Jesus himself. It can act out the will to hear and to obey.

The physical character and appearance of the Bible, the way it is carried and handled, even opened, are important. The use, especially in a funeral home, of the Bible normally used in a congregation's services, for example, communicates a sense of the sacredness of the Word and a feeling for church and tradition better than does the use of the leaflet or small service book.

The phrases used to introduce the readings should not be unthinkingly chosen or spoken in an offhand, slipshod way. At the same time, they should be simple and brief, such as, "Hear the Word of God in a reading from _____," or "A Reading from _____." And the people may answer, "Thanks be to God." As previously noted, lections may be read by others than the pastor. In fact, reading by members of the deceased family or by friends, even if emotionally difficult for them, should be encouraged. Who can know what such an action may mean for those who read and for those who hear, at the moment itself or in days to come?

Music may be offered between the lections at the pastor's discretion, although the use of Psalm 23 between Old and New Testament lections is felt to be virtually essential. This psalm should not be thought of as taking the place of the Old Testament lection; rather, it functions as an act of praise. Preferably, it should be sung (or, if necessary, said) by the people, standing, perhaps using Hymns 67 or 68 in the hymnal. Musical settings of other biblical passages—numbers 846, 847 in *The Book of Hymns*—should also be considered. This music should not be of such a character as to clash with the proclamation. At the same time, all music is evocative, and the dynamic meanings it suggests may proclaim the gospel more effectively than the rational content of the musical text would lead one to expect.

The people's sense of time and of movement also needs to be considered. A sequence of three or four passages of Scripture, plus sermon, without interruption, may simply be too many words; the people's attention may lag. The length of the passages, of course, needs to be borne in mind. Yet, clock time here is not as important as the people's sense of liturgical and psychological time. As a general rule, music at this point should be sung by the people, be organic to the movement of the service, and be theologically consistent with the gospel of death and resurrection.

[Naming]

This optional act is intended to keep proclamation related to the real situation of the people in a ministering way.

Its purpose is to personalize the service by singling out and lifting up the individual, human selfhood of the deceased, and by identifying—implicitly or explicitly—the relationships of the deceased to the mourners. It may be part of, or immediately follow, the sermon. It may be used separately or joined to the act of witness that follows. An appropriate memorial or obituary-type statement may be prepared in advance and read by the pastor or someone else, or signs and symbols described below under Witness may be used. Such an act locates the deceased in the communities—geographical, familial, educational, religious, social, vocational (such as a business, trade, or profession)—that significantly shaped that life now ended. The act can recognize particular achievements. It can be a means of summarily reviewing and cherishing the life of the deceased, and then of letting go, reinforcing the finality of death even while evoking marvel before the color and individuality of human life. For a Christian, it reminds again of the name connected with Baptism, at which time the deceased was buried and raised with Christ and engrafted as an individual member into the body of Christ's church.

Naming can also be cared for in other ways—in the prayers and sentences as indicated in this order, at the services on the Sunday following the funeral, and on All Saints' and Memorial Days. This act clearly lends itself to use in memorial services and on other occasions, although in revised form and under a different title.

[Witness]

The heading here should be carefully noted because it includes the purpose of the activity as well as the name of it and can therefore caution participants about lapsing into spurious eulogy with all its dangers. The act of witness is intended to direct thought to the deceased, but within the context of God, God's grace, thanksgiving for grace, Christian faith, hope, love, and Christian joy. This context is vital. The value of personalizing the service in a natural human way is retained, but the personalizing is set within these larger meanings that constitute a form of proclamation.

As a matter of fact, the nature and function of eulogy may need to be rethought. If there is dishonest eulogy, there is also such a thing as truthful eulogy. Understood as "tribute" or "appreciation," eulogy is essentially thankfulness, and surely thankfulness to God—even when verbally addressed to people—is not out of place in proclamation. Further, the qualities of the personality and life of the deceased for which thanks is given are said to have "graced" the lives of the survivors. This does not mean, of course, that the deceased is idealized. Rather, all that is appreciated is gratefully acknowledged as a gift from God. Those invited to offer witness should have this explained to them in advance.

The emotional poignancy of this action—like that of naming—involves risk. But risks may be taken. Psychologically, the expression of feelings is important. Theologically, such signs as words, objects, gestures, enable people to act out before God and with one another their thanksgiving, faith, hope, love, joy. One kind of sign is the brief verbal tribute, preferably arranged for and prepared in advance. Another sign is the traditional Peace—verbal exchange, handclasp, silent embrace. Flowers—perhaps of the kind most loved by the deceased—may be brought in at this point in the service. Brief passages from favorite books or poems of the deceased may be read, favorite pictures displayed. Some symbol of the vocation or accomplishments of the deceased—a tool, a garment, an award, a product of the deceased's work—may be commented on. Selected messages and tributes from mourners unable to be present can be read. People who have traveled from a considerable distance may be recognized; their travel is itself a witness. A sheaf of wheat whose grain must fall into the ground and die before it can bring forth life may be silently laid on the coffin. When appropriate, the death mask of the deceased may be viewed. Imagination and faith may suggest other signs.

The pastor may incorporate in the announcement of this action the words of St. Paul:

Praise be to the God and Father of our Lord Jesus Christ, the all-merciful Father, the God whose consolation never fails us!

He comforts us in all our troubles, so that we in turn may be able to comfort others in any trouble of theirs and to share with them the consolation we ourselves receive from God. (II Corinthians 1:3-4, NEB)

A congregational hymn or song appropriately concludes this action; it regathers the people and sustains the movement of the service.

The act of witness, like the preceding naming, can readily be modified for use at a memorial service or other occasion. An alternative occasion for the action of witness may be a brief service of prayer and thanksgiving at the viewing of the body at a time other than the funeral.

C. Responses and Offering of Life

A Liturgical Perspective

The phrase "offering of Life" is related to other similar terms—committal, commendation, dedication, oblation, sacrifice. These are not quite synonyms, and the forms of expression they take in Christian worship also vary. But they all have in common that they refer to the God of Jesus Christ as the end beyond all other ends unto whom we live and die, to faith's insight that our human destiny is in this God, and to a liturgical act that declares this faith. The concluding section of the service focuses on this reality.

Understood in this way, the responses and offering of life are the culmination of a natural movement and momentum that seems to operate in the service. Initiated in the gathering, it progresses through proclamation and praise and issues with a certain inevitability in the responses and offering of life. This order parallels the basic pattern in *Word and Table* and the liturgies of many other churches. Of course, response in the form of offering occurs throughout the service and in acts within acts. Besides that, neither the funeral nor Christian worship in general should ever be designed to produce spiritual states and psychological experiences at prescribed moments. Who can ever say where offering really occurs or what form it will take? Yet, provision for offering of life needs

61

to be intentional and definite. Without it the motion of worship is not complete—spiritually, ethically, or psychologically—and the proclamation of the gospel as death and resurrection is not fulfilled.

Worshipers may or may not perceive the depth of meaning this action holds at the time it is performed or its implications for their existence. Outwardly, offering may appear to be an action willed and performed by the people themselves. Originally and inwardly, however, it is caused by the action of God. It is response to divine grace already active on conscious and subconscious levels of personality. It is God acting in, with, and under the outward forms of human action. In this deep sense the worshiper's offering of life is really God's raising to life. Nothing less than resurrection can come to pass. Encounter with death becomes transformed into an experience of newness of life now for the living, identifying marks of which are often the breaking of the grip of guilt and fear, a sense of healing, greater sensitiveness, a saner vision of reality, a longer-range view of time that can even become a sense of eternity, a renewal of willed obedience, a certain peace. In short, through the offering of life as a union with God as one's destiny, the self is reconstituted. This union alone matches the fatefulness of our human experience of death.

A succession of actions provides for this experience of union. The creed can offer the people's joyful trust in God's saving action in Jesus Christ as the event on which they take their stand and by which they are prepared to live and die. Intercessory prayer offers the people's love for one another and for all who mourn. The prayer of commendation, or the committal service, offers the life of the deceased and the life of the people. The prayer of thanksgiving, culminating in the Lord's Prayer, parallels the Great Thanksgiving of Holy Communion in offering the gratitude of the people for their creation and redemption. Through these means and moments the people present themselves to God, souls and bodies, to be a holy and living sacrifice to him. The result for them can be an experience of destiny, a coming home, a restoration of life.

As noted, the offering of life is also provided for in alternative ways. Thus, *if the committal service* normally used at the grave or cremation *is included* in shortened form *as part of the Service of Death and Resurrection, it replaces this entire section,* "The Offering of Life," and becomes the climax and conclusion of the service. Similarly, *Holy Communion* may be administered at the indicated place in the service. While the sacrament holds many meanings as explained below, it is a unique and powerful act of self-offering. *If it is included, it replaces the prayer of thanksgiving* ("O God of love . . .") *and the Lord's Prayer given in the funeral text,* and the service ends with a hymn, dismissal, and blessing.

[*The Creed*]

If included as an option, the creed is to be understood and used here—as well as in the church's worship generally—as a celebration of salvation events, not as a statement of doctrine. Originally, all the professions of faith in the New Testament bore this character. They were expressions of joy in the lordship of Christ known through the Jesus of history, doxological rather than didactic. Only later, largely in response to controversy, did creeds come to be seen as confining. The Apostles' Creed, printed here in the ecumenical translation of the International Consultation on English texts, functions in this way. As the worshiper's response to proclamation, it is a reoffering of heart and mind. It remembers the faith of Baptism. It singles out and avows the death and resurrection of Jesus Christ as decisive for one's destiny.

If used, the posture of standing is the only proper one.

[*Prayers*]

This part of the order reflects the conviction that the service is best thought of as prayer-centered rather than as sermon-centered. It also constitutes the climax of the service in general and the action of offering in particular.

Other prayers may, of course, be substituted for those in the text. Also, there is nothing ironclad about the sequence of intercession, commendation, thanksgiving. The use of intercessory prayer, however, seems almost inescapable here. Intercessory prayer is probably as tender and bold an act of love as there is. By its very nature it is intensely mutual. It rightly enlists sympathy and taxes sensitivity and imagination. Here the true needs of those who mourn, not merely superficial needs, are apprehended and named, needs such as light, strength, forgiveness, peace, love. There are others. Intercession is also a bold act of faith; probably there is none bolder. Trust in God's nature as active love is audaciously put forth. Intercession is also the church functioning as church. It has been "called out" for just this purpose. The priesthood of all believers is here experienced and declared. In intercession, the prayer of the church on earth mystically joins with the praise and prayer of the church in heaven.

The prayer of commendation, "O God, all that you have given . . . ," serves several purposes. It is a forthright offering to God of the deceased through word, metaphor, gesture. It is meant to communicate a sense of finality and termination, a kind of last act of love. It names God as the giver and end of life and reminds anew in whom all life finds its destiny. It correctly defines resurrection as God's raising us, not as our raising of ourselves. It links the offering of the life of the survivors with the act of offering of the deceased, and invokes the first and greatest commandment as the condition of the new life into which God raises his people. It expresses the Christian hope of joy in God's kingdom after death. It suggests the spirit of what has been called the Christian prayer beyond all prayers, Jesus' final words, "Father, into thy hands I commend my spirit."

Thanksgiving or doxology is fittingly the first and the last word in Christian prayer. In this setting, prayer voices God's love in creation and in redemption as the reality on which faith takes its ultimate stand. Thanksgiving for this love frames everything else, even suffering and sorrow. Symbolic meanings from the homely texture of everyday life, but even more the remembrance (*anamnesis*): "Do this in remembrance of me" of Jesus' life, death, resurrection evoke such thanksgiving.

The Lord's Prayer prayed in unison appropriately concludes this part of the service. It gathers up all other prayers and is probably the most universal bond of faith. Its final ascription of power and glory, with the words "forever and ever," seals all else with a doxology of invincible faith and joy. It is omitted here only if the Order for Communion, which embodies it, is used.

The prayers of intercession, commendation, and thanksgiving may need to be rethought for services for the unchurched or non-Christian. The assumptions of faith underlying such services may not be valid. Or, they may be more valid than first supposed. Pastoral sensitivity is very important here.

[Holy Communion]

Provision for the Lord's Supper at the funeral may seem strange to United Methodists, and in congregations where such celebration would be perceived as so incongruous as to be disabling, it should not be conducted. Neither should it be celebrated at a funeral for the unchurched or the non-Christian. Only after consultation with the family of the deceased, or with the deceased before death, and in accord with a congregation's guidelines for worship, should it be celebrated. Here, the meanings—true or incomplete or distorted—that Communion has come to hold for people across the years need to be pastorally discerned and weighed alongside liturgical integrity.

In educating the people and deciding the question, it should be borne in mind that, from the church's beginning, the Eucharist was probably celebrated by the congregation at the time of a Christian's death. From the third century on, it was celebrated both at the grave and in congregational assembly. Probably, the original impulse was the natural wish of the living to maintain union with departed relatives and friends, the Eucharist being the deepest expression of that union. Union of the faithful was in and through Christ, not—as so often thought today, even by church people—through spiritualist contact with the dead. Later, the purpose of the funeral Eucharist changed and became more propitiatory, issuing in the corruptions against which the Reformers protested. In our ecumenical age these controversies have largely been resolved, and appreciation of the common sacramental heritage that predated them has grown to embrace celebration of the funeral Eucharist. Free-church Protestants appear to have been slower in realizing this than other denominations.

This appreciation is of course part of the movement toward restoring the full, ancient unity of the liturgy of Word and Table as normative for a congregation's life. The question becomes, then, Are not both Word and Meal similarly desirable at the funeral if the gospel is to be proclaimed in its fullness? Does a service of song, lections, sermon, prayers, without Meal, suffice? Often the answer will be that it does.

Nevertheless, it should be remembered that Holy Communion is proclamation of the gospel message of death and resurrection *par excellence* with all of its overtones of penitence and faith, of brokenness and healing, of sorrow and joy. In this sense the Sacrament is as evangelical—indeed as evangelistic—an act as the church performs. Worship in the character of Meal here re-presents better than it does anywhere else the Supper Jesus ate with his disciples the night before his death. It recalls further the meals he ate with his disciples at which he disclosed his risen life. It is a foretaste of the supper of the Lamb which he promised to eat with his own in the day of his kingdom. At the same time, response to the message of death and resurrection is inevitably the thankful offering and reoffering by the people of their life, their being taken up into Jesus' destiny as their own, their sense of oneness with all who through him have lived and died, their nourishment with his bread and wine for the burdens they shall bear, and the taking up of his cross as their way unto life.

If Holy Communion is celebrated, the brief order in the service booklet is suggested. This replaces the prayer of thanksgiving and the Lord's Prayer in the usual order. All present who wish to partake should be invited and served. Family members and friends of the deceased may assist in the distribution. Grouping of the people by tables and table dismissals is not necessary or encourged. Increasingly, congregations are finding that going forward, moving past one or more places where the bread and cup are given, receiving Communion standing—probably the most ancient custom— and returning to one's seat for personal prayer combine reverence and efficiency.

[Hymn]

The concluding song should promptly follow the prayers or the Sacrament, and the service should move with dispatch to its conclusion. Almost certainly this song will be a congregational hymn. Alternatively, the Doxology may be appropriate, or possibly a chant such as the *Nunc Dimittis* or the closing sung prayer "God Be in My Head, and in My Understanding" (Number 813 in *The Book of Hymns*).

[Dismissal with Blessing]

The term "dismissal" means "sending" and rightly incorporates into the funeral the congregation's missional nature. The congregation has been gathered as those who have been sent, and they are sent forth as those who have been gathered. Further, the death and resurrection motif of the service is the same motif the Christian is to live out in the world, and service to God in assembly for worship continues in service to people everywhere.

The term "blessing" has more of the meaning of "sealing." The people bless God, but even more they are blessed by God. That is, they are once more marked as God's, established in God, covered with God's grace and held in God's peace. The benedictions printed in the text (Hebrews 13:20-21; Philippians 4:7) convey these two meanings, preferably in this sequence. Alternate dismissals and blessings are found in Resources. A service as intensely Christian as a Service of Death and Resurrection should be concluded with distinct Christian and Trinitarian blessings and dismissals taken from the New Testament. The dismissal given in the order specifically refers to the death and resurrection of Jesus and to the graces flowing from it that equip the Christian for service. These sentences should be spoken by the pastor face to face with the congregation, not from the rear of the church, the congregation preferably standing.

If there is a recessional it may form in approximately the same order as the processional. If not, the pastor may take up a position before the coffin and precede it as it is borne from the place of the service to the hearse, again carried by pallbearers. The pastor should consult with the funeral director before the funeral about procedures at this point. Music may be played or sung during the departure of the people. There is much to be said, however, for not having music here and instead concluding the service in silence.

D. Committal Service

A Liturgical Perspective

The word "committal" in the title of this service holds several meanings. Functionally, it refers to the disposition of the body of the deceased. Sociologically, it denotes a communal act of respect and homage to the deceased. Psychologically, it implies a facing of physical death and a final letting go. Theologically, it reflects the Christian vision of things seen and unseen. Here the people give thanks to God for the deceased, and pray for the dead and the living. Especially here the people offer to God the life of the deceased and their own lives. All these meanings mingle liturgically, and the committal service becomes a ritual of confrontation with destiny.

Thus understood, the committal service recapitulates some of the meanings of the Service of Death and Resurrection, particularly the offering of life. If it is held separately from the funeral service, pastoral judgment will determine how long and how substantive the committal service should be. Generally, committal services are too brief, especially when an interval has elapsed between funeral and committal and when numbers of people attend the committal who were not present at the funeral. Options in this committal service enable it to be expanded. On occasion, the committal is included as part of the funeral service. If so, the order should be shortened as provided for, and substituted for the last section (Responses and Offering of Life) of A Service of Death and Resurrection. If Communion is celebrated, the committal should follow in shortened form. If military, civic, or fraternal rites are conducted, they should follow the committal.

Clearly, the poignancy of this moment calls for great sensitivity both liturgically and pastorally. The very variety of occasions of committal—grave burial, cremation, interment of ashes, entombment—underscores this need. Thus the rubric, "The Pastor should preside," holds particular significance although not in any clerical sense. Others may participate in conducting the service, and of course the wishes of the family, as well as local custom and tradition, should be borne in mind. The fatefulness with which liturgy is charged at this moment, however, is too great for the service to be determined by other than a pastor—ordained or unordained—responsible for acting in the name of Christ and the church. Only in cases of genuine necessity or of careful choice should anyone other than the pastor who conducted the funeral service preside at the committal. An important part of the pastor's responsibility is to take particular care with ceremonial and symbol because they hold such deep religious meaning here; indeed they will likely speak more powerfully than words. Spiritual intention, honesty, simplicity, naturalness—these are the criteria to go by. Because of the significance of ceremonial and symbol, the pastor in charge should come to a clear understanding in advance with the funeral director concerning all parts of the ceremony.

In most situations, the people will *gather* informally at the grave. Since location of the grave (or crematorium), weather, numbers in attendance, and custom affect the physical movement of the people, the manner of gathering and the arrangement of the assembly may need to be adjusted. Possibly an informal processional of all the people—led by the pastor, followed by the pallbearers carrying the coffin, and then by the family—may voice Christian meaning better than detaining the people until the coffin is in place. Too smooth or self-conscious or furtive attempts to lessen the starkness of the occasion, while usually well-meant, are false. The very earthiness, even unexpected awkwardness of physical movement in procession and in carrying and placing the coffin can contribute honesty and reality to the moment. The people likewise need not be herded into rows; an informal circle around the grave, for example, may express Christian meaning better. The pastor should stand at the head of the grave and of the unlowered coffin.

The *opening sentences* in the text may be spoken in whole or in part. They embody a sequence of devotion that contrapuntally voices the gospel of death and resurrection. They include a portion of a ninth-century antiphon in the Episcopal *Book of Common Prayer (Proposed),* Psalm 124:8, Romans 8:11, selected verses from I Corinthians 15, and Psalm 16:9, 11. They should be spoken to the people loudly enough to be heard.

The *prayer* that follows is revised from traditional sources and links the act of committal of the deceased with the self-offering of the people. If copies of the service are available for the people's use, the prayer should be prayed in unison.

The *lections* (I Peter 1:3-9 and John 12:23-26) are optional. They proclaim the gospel promise of resurrection, but not without qualification; faith and obedience still are overtones.

The sentences of *committal* open with Jesus' final prayer from the cross, name the deceased by Christian (or first) name, and include elements of the church's traditional liturgies. The concluding sentences are from Revelation 14:13. The asterisked alternate words of committal for other graveside services are self-explanatory; in particular, the phrase "the elements" is appropriate for cremation.

As the heading indicates, the pastor at this moment faces the coffin, not necessarily the people, turning if need be to do so. It is desirable that the coffin be lowered at this particular moment, if possible beginning at the words, "This body we commit." Less preferably, the coffin may be lowered immediately after the people have gathered, or immediately after the benediction. Whatever the choice of time, it should not be to lower the coffin surreptitiously after the mourners have left. At cremation, on the other hand, the coffin should remain in place until the mourners have left, rather than being removed with a mechanical affect.

If possible, real earth from the grave—not flowers, nor sand from envelopes—should be cast on the coffin by the pastor, not by the funeral director. Simultaneously, earth may be cast upon the coffin by family members or other mourners if desired. Earth or flowers may be dropped upon the lowered coffin after the benediction as a symbol of respect, committal, and farewell by other mourners if desired. Arrangements for gesture and symbol here should be planned in advance with the funeral director and family, although spontaneous expressions should not be ruled out.

The choice of *prayers* after the committal depends on the needs of the people, on the desired length of the service, on whether the committal service is held separately from the funeral service or included in it, and on the pastor's liturgical instinct and sensitivity. Other prayers than those printed may of course be used. Prayers appropriate for distinctive occasions are found in Resources. Prayers from the concluding section of the Service of Death and Resurrection may also be considered. Extemporary prayer prepared by the pastor also is not out of place. The first four prayers suggested here are largely revisions taken from the church's traditional liturgies. They include thanksgiving, intercession for the deceased and the mourners, and petition for God's grace, and constitute a unity. The last prayer combines these elements. Places in the prayers where the first name of the deceased is spoken and where masculine or feminine pronouns need to be inserted should be noted. The people respond with the "Amen." The Lord's Prayer is optional.

The option of a *hymn or song* should be considered if it is judged that the service will not be unduly prolonged and if music here is not emotionally overwhelming. Sometimes music sung by the people can fittingly close the service; often one or two stanzas from a familiar hymn, or a doxology, are sufficient.

The first blessing (Jude 24) stresses the character of God as able to guard the Christian amidst frailty and vicissitude until the day of Christ's coming. As ascription and doxology, it also offers the entire service as an act of worship to God. The text is taken mainly from the King James Version because of its poetic quality. The second blessing (John 14:1-3) voices Jesus' matchless promise of peace. It is followed by the familiar and beloved Trinitarian grace uniquely appropriate for closing a Christian Service.

The pastor faces the people in giving the blessing, using whatever gesture is felt to be liturgically appropriate, perhaps signing the people with the Christian sign of the cross. Then, usually though not always, the pastor's physical movement should signal a definite conclusion to the service, probably by approaching relatives or other mourners in quiet farewell or by accompanying them as they leave. On occasion, however, if the emotional intensity is not too great and if weather and other circumstances permit, pastor and people may wish to tarry and to greet and visit with one another in a natural way.

III. Additional Resources

A. Words of Grace and Sentences

1. For General Use in the Service or Elsewhere

We do not live to ourselves, and we do not die to ourselves. If we live, we live to the Lord; and if we die, we die to the Lord. So then, whether we live or whether we die, we are the Lord's. To this end Christ died and lived again, that he might be Lord both of the dead and the living. (Romans 14:7-9) And he died for all, that those who live might live no longer for themselves but for him who for their sake died and rose again. (II Corinthians 5:15 RSV) When Christ who is our life shall appear, then you will also appear with him in glory. (Colossians 3:4)

I love the Lord because he has heard my voice and my supplications. Because he has inclined his ear to me, therefore I will call on him as long as I live. The cords of death bound me; the pangs of the grave laid hold on me; I suffered distress and anguish. Then I called on the name of the Lord: "O Lord, I beseech thee, save my life!" Gracious is the Lord, and righteous. . . . I was brought low and he saved me. . . . Precious in the sight of the Lord is the death of his saints. O Lord, I am your servant. . . . I will offer to you the sacrifice of thanksgiving and call on the name of the Lord. I will pay my vows to the Lord in the presence of all his people. (Psalm 116:1-5, 6*b*, 15-16*a*, 17-18)

The eternal God is our dwelling place, and underneath are the everlasting arms. (Deuteronomy 33:27) God is our refuge and strength, a very present help in trouble. (Psalm 46:1 RSV) Know that the Lord is God. He has made us and we are his own. We are his people, the flock which he shepherds. . . . Give thanks to him and bless his name; for the

Lord is good, his love is everlasting, and his truth endures to all generations. (Psalm 100:3, 4b-5 NEB adapted)

I know that my Redeemer lives and that he shall stand upon the earth at the Last Day; and though my flesh shall have turned to dust, yet shall I see God. I shall see him for myself; these eyes shall behold him, I myself and no other. (Job 19:25-27) The Lord is my light and my salvation; whom shall I fear? The Lord is the strength of my life; of whom shall I be afraid? . . . I believe that I shall see the goodness of the Lord in the land of the living! Wait for the Lord. Be of good courage, and he shall strengthen your heart. Wait, I say, on the Lord. (Psalm 27:1, 13-14)

---

2. At the Service for a Child or Youth

The Lord is merciful and gracious, slow to anger and abounding in steadfast love. . . . As a father pities his children, so the Lord pities those who fear him. For he knows our frame; he remembers that we are dust. . . . But the steadfast love of the Lord is from everlasting to everlasting upon those who fear him, and his righteousness to children's children. (Psalm 103:8, 13-14, 17 RSV)

Jesus said, let the children come to me and forbid them not, for of such is the kingdom of heaven. . . . And he took them in his arms and blessed them. (Mark 10:14, 16) The Lamb in the midst of the throne will be their shepherd, and he will guide them to springs of living water; and God will wipe away every tear from their eyes. (Revelation 7:17 RSV)

---

3. For an Untimely or Tragic Death

Blessed be the God who comforts us in all our sorrows, so that we can offer others, in their sorrows, the consolation that we have received from God ourselves. (II Corinthians 1:3a, 4) He may bring us sorrow, but his love for us is sure and strong. (Lamentations 3:32) Cast your burden on the Lord, and he will sustain you. (Psalm 55:22a RSV)

ADDITIONAL RESOURCES

B. Prayers

Prayers may be selected from these resources and joined with appropriate Scripture lessons to compose a very brief service for a viewing, or for an informal service in the home of a family or elsewhere.

Some of these prayers are original. Others have borrowed a thought, a sentence, or a phrase from another source but recast or combined it with other material to make a substantially new prayer. Others are revisions of prayers taken from the church's ecumenical heritage of prayer, as noted. All are presented for use either as written or as models for the pastor's adaptation.

1. For General Use

Lord God, we pray to you, the source of all that is. You hold us in being; without you we could not be. Before we were born, before time began, before the universe came into being, you were. When time is finished, when this world is no more, you still will be. Nothing can finally deny you. Nothing can destroy you. Before the silent mystery of your being we kneel in awe and in prayer.

Yet you have spoken to us. Out of silence your Word has come. You have spoken, and given form and beauty to our world. You have spoken, and given purpose to human life. You have spoken, and redeemed us from our sins. You have spoken, and freed us from death.

Lord Jesus Christ, living Word, speak to us now. Unite us with the eternal purpose. Take away our burden of failure and guilt. Conquer death in our hearts. Speak, and help us hear, we pray.

God forever, your love is stronger than death. For the hope in you that faith gives, and for all our people who have laid hold on that hope, we praise you. Especially we lift up our hearts in thankfulness for the life of *(name)* whom you have taken to yourself. We thank you for all your goodness to _____; for all that _____ meant to those who loved _____; for everything in _____ life that reflected your grace. We

75

thank you that _____ sins are forgiven, all suffering is past, and that united with all those _____ loved who have gone before us, _____ has entered into your joy.

Hold us and all who mourn today in your love. Let sorrow have its way with us, but let it not overwhelm us nor turn us against you. Work in us your will. Set our hands again to our tasks. And bring us at last, in the communion of all your people, to your home where we long to be. Through Jesus Christ our Lord. **Amen.**[1]

Eternal God, in death you hold us in life. When life ends you bring us to a new beginning. You created the earth and the heavens. In exodus and exile you saved your people. You raised up Jesus from death, and sent his Spirit as Lord and Giver of life. Help us in this time of death to know you as our God and ourselves as your people, and to begin again to live this day and every day in the life you give to us in Jesus Christ our Lord.

Thanks be to you, O God, for the victory of Jesus Christ. We thank you it was a real victory won by blood amid our human struggle. We thank you it was a victory of courage over fear; of good will over evil; of forgiveness over sin; of faith over death. We pray for Christ's victory in our minds and hearts today. In its truth, save us from illusion and despair. By its power, raise us above immoral and selfish living. Through its grace, conquer death and the fear of death in our hearts.

Lord God of all flesh, you give life and you summon in death. Into your keeping we give *(name)*; _____ life, _____ mind, _____ desires, _____ deeds, _____ labors, _____ body—all. In you, ever, may _____ live and have _____ being. Hold _____, and hold us all, ever more, in our going out and our coming in, in our returning and in our departing. **Amen.**[2]

How unsearchable are your ways, O God, how deep your thoughts! Your will in our life holds such mystery. Yet in all your dealings with us, whether of joy or of pain, you would bring us to know you. Help us to value each sorrow and happiness not because it denies or gives us what we want but because it brings us nearer you. In every trial we trust your love for us, in every darkness that you are leading us, in every death that you will give us life, as in his death you gave life to your Son our Saviour, Jesus Christ. **Amen.**[3]

Lord, God, you give life to us and then you take it away. You hide it in the secret of death, and then purify it into eternal life. Look upon us in our sorrow for this life taken from us, and gather our pain into your peace. Cleanse with your Holy Spirit our memories, our broodings, our doubtings, and hallow all in your purpose for us. Teach us to consider that we too must die, and until that hour comes, hold us steady in our hope in you of which never will we be ashamed. We pray through Jesus Christ our Lord. **Amen.**[4]

Loving God, you comfort all who mourn. In the light of our Saviour's life, we lift up to you our hearts. We thank you for that true light which shines even in our darkness. We thank you for all who have walked therein, and especially for those dear to us in whom we have seen your grace and truth. May we know that they are with you, and that when our earthly days have come to an end, it is not that our service of you and of one another may cease, but that it may begin anew. Make us glad in all who have faithfully lived and faithfully died. And gather us at the last into the communion of all who have trusted in you and sought to do your will; through Jesus Christ our Lord. **Amen.**[5]

We give thanks to you, O Lord our God, for all your servants and witnesses of time past: Abraham the father of believers; Moses, Samuel, Isaiah and all the prophets; John the Baptist, the forerunner; Mary, the mother of our Lord; Peter, Paul and all the apostles; martyrs and saints in every age and land; and those of our own household of faith gathered from us. In your mercy, give us, with them, hope in your salvation and in the promise of life in your eternal kingdom;

through Christ our Lord, our resurrection, and our life. **Amen.**[6]

Almighty God, you have knit your chosen people together in one communion in the mystical body of your Son, Jesus Christ our Lord. Give to our whole Church in heaven and on earth your light and your peace. Grant that all who have been baptized into Christ's death and resurrection, may die to sin and rise to newness of life, and that through the gate of death we may pass with him to our joyful resurrection. **Amen.**[7]

Grant us, God, above all things that can be desired, to rest in you, and in you to have our peace. You alone are true peace to our souls, you our only rest. You have made us for yourself, and our hearts are restless until they rest in you. Deepen in us the sense of your eternity, that from you we may gather strength for our trials, comfort in our grief, and peace for our way unto the end. **Amen.**[8]

Give faith and courage, Lord, to all who mourn, that with good heart they may meet the trials and tasks that lie ahead. Let them not sorrow as those without hope, but in thankfulness for your goodness in years past, trust also in your strength through the years to come. In Christ's Name we pray. **Amen.**

Jesus our Friend, you wept at the grave of Lazarus, you know all our sorrows. Behold our tears and bind up the wounds of our hearts. Through the mystery of pain, bring us into closer communion with you and with one another. Raise us from death into life. And grant in your mercy, that with *(name)* who has passed within the veil, we may come to live with you and with all whom we love in our Father's home. **Amen.**[9]

Lord Jesus Christ, who didst abide with thy disciples when it was toward evening and the day was far spent: Tarry with us, we pray Thee, as we enter into the shadows, assuring us by Thy mercy that thou wilt stay with us to the end. **Amen.**[10]

O God, King Eternal, whose light divides the day from the night and turns the shadow of death into the morning: Drive from us all wrong desires, bring our hearts to keep your law, and guide our feet into the way of peace; that, having done your will with cheerfulness during the day, we may, when night comes, rejoice to give you thanks; through Jesus Christ our Lord. **Amen.**[11]

Come, O Lord, with your healing, and comfort all who wait in the long watches of the night. Quiet every troubled heart. Soften the pain of those who grieve for their loved ones. Help them to know that you are ever faithful, ever strong, keeping watch above your own; through Jesus Christ our Lord. **Amen.**[12]

Lord, we commend to your goodness all those who desire or need our prayers; those dear to us whom we name in our hearts before you; those forgotten by us but dear to you; those unknown to us but known to you. With your peace guard them, and in your love keep them, now and forever. **Amen.**[13]

Lord Jesus Christ, you have given us grace at this time with one accord to make our common supplication, and have promised that when two or three are agreed together in your Name you will grant their requests: Fulfill now, O Lord, our desires and petitions as may be best for us; granting us in this world knowledge of your truth, and in the world to come life everlasting; through your mercy, O Christ, to whom with the Father and the Holy Spirit be honor and glory forever more. **Amen.**[14]

---

2. At the Service for a Child or Youth

God our Father, your love gave us life and your care never fails. Yours is the beauty of childhood, and yours the ight that shines in the face of age. For all whom you have given to be dear to our hearts, we thank you, and especially for this child you have taken to yourself. Into the arms of your love we give _____ soul, remembering Jesus' words, "Let the children come unto me, for of such is the kingdom of heaven." Unto your love also we commend the sorrowing parents and family. Pity them as a father his children; comfort them as a mother her little ones. As their love follows their hearts' treasure, help them to trust that love they once have known is never lost, that the child taken from their sight lives forever in your presence. Into your hands we also give ourselves, our regret for whatever more we might have been or done, our need to trust you more and to pray, all our struggle for a better life. Comfort us all. Keep tender and true the love in which we hold each other. Let not our longing for you ever cease. May things unseen and eternal grow more real for us, more full of meaning, that in our living and dying you may be our peace. **Amen.**[15]

God our Father, whose face the angels of little children do always behold in heaven, comfort us in the assurance that a life that once has been made dear to us cannot be lost; that ties broken in this world are still preserved in your love that first made them ours; and that the powers we would have helped train in this child taken from us, are now unfolding in your very presence. Save us from letting the limits of our understanding, limit our faith. If we, unworthy as we are, yet seek good things for our children here, how much more will your love bless them with all good things in your heavenly kingdom. Deepen our faith even amidst the bitterness of our grief. And give us grace so to conform our lives to the innocence and trust of our children here, that we may be united again with them in your eternal home. **Amen.**[16]

O Lord, who keepest little children in this present world, and because of their innocence holdest them close to thyself in the life to come, receive in peace the soul of thy child *(name)*, for you have said, "Of such is my kingdom in heaven." **Amen.**[17]

3. An Untimely or Tragic Death

God of us all, we thank you for Christ's grace through which we pray to you in this dark hour. A life we love has been torn from us. Expectations the years once held have vanished.[18] The mystery of death has stricken us. O God, you know the lives we live and the deaths we die—woven so strangely of purpose and of chance, of reason and the irrational, of strength and of frailty, of happiness and of pain.

Into your hands we commend the soul of *(name)*. No mortal life you have made is without eternal meaning. No earthly fate is beyond your redeeming. Through your grace that can do far more than we can think or imagine, fulfill in _____ your purpose that reaches beyond time and death. Lead _____ from strength to strength, and fit _____ for love and service in your kingdom.

Into your hands also we commit our lives. You alone, God, make us to dwell in safety. Whom, finally, have we on earth or in heaven but you? Help us to know the measure of our days, and how frail we are. Hold us in your keeping. Forgive us our sins. Save our minds from despair and our hearts from fear. And guard and guide us with your peace. **Amen.**

Everlasting God, in Christ's resurrection you turned the disciples' despair into triumph, their sorrow into joy. Give us faith to believe that every good that seems to be overcome by evil, and every love that seems to be buried in death, shall rise again to life eternal. Through Jesus Christ who lives and reigns with you forever more. **Amen.**[19]

Almighty God, in your keeping there is shelter from the storm, and in your mercy there is comfort for the sorrows of life. Hear now our prayer for those who mourn and are heavy laden. Give to them strength to bear and do your will. Lighten their darkness with your love. Enable them to see beyond the things of this mortal world the promise of the eternal. Help them to know that your care enfolds all your people, that you are our refuge and strength, and that underneath are your everlasting arms. **Amen.**[20]

---

4. At the Service for the Non-Christian or Unchurched

Eternal God, you have set us in this vast universe, and in the mystery of time whose currents bear us more swiftly than we know to what we call death. When we try to grasp your purpose in it all, we confess our ignorance even as we marvel in wonder. Yet we believe you created us. You gave us minds to think and hearts to seek. You gave us wills to decide and work to do. All life is within your design, and in Christ you have shown us what our life can be.[21]

We thank you for *(name)*, and for all the goodness, beauty and trust in _____ life that fulfilled your purpose for _____, and that made our lives richer for _____ presence. We thank you for love given and for love received; for defeats mastered and tasks well done; for faithful friendship; and for all graces of soul and character that endeared _____ to us. Keep tender in our hearts these memories. Grateful for this life you have given us, help us now to give it back into your hands, knowing that *(name)* and all whose faces we see no more are in your care and keeping.

Grant us the help of your Spirit in the days to come. Especially uphold those who will most keenly feel the pain of this death and this parting. Patiently heal their sorrow. Free them from burdens and sins of the past. Strengthen the love that binds them to one another. Help them, and help us all, to discern the meaning of our years. Let not the sorrow of death rob us of the joy of life. Whatever light may shine or shadow fall, give us a brave heart, and faith to make of everything temporal a path that leads to life eternal. In your Name we pray. **Amen.**[22]

Lord God, we commend to you all who have departed this life trusting in you, that they may pass through the valley of the shadow and enter into your rest. Look favorably, also, upon those whose lives were saddened and crushed, who scarcely knew your grace because of our unconcern and want of love. Lay their sins to our charge, that our guilt may bring us to repent, to do justice, and to walk more humbly with you our God. Grant mercy also to those who have departed this life in ignorance or defiance of you. We plead for them in the spirit of him who prayed, "Father, forgive them, for they know not what they do," our Saviour and your Son, Jesus Christ our Lord. **Amen.**[23]

Almighty and everlasting God, you are always more ready to hear than we are to pray, to give more than we desire or deserve. Pour out upon us your great mercy, forgiving us those things of which our conscience is afraid, and giving us those good things we are not worthy to ask, but through Jesus Christ our Lord. **Amen.**[24]

Teach us, Lord, not to hold on to life too tightly. Teach us to hold it lightly; not carelessly, but lightly. You have given life as a gift to enjoy while we have it, and to be let go gracefully when our time comes. Your gift is great, but you the Giver are greater still. In you is life that never dies, and with you are joys forever more. **Amen.**[25]

Almighty God, you give us new life, new hope, and new opportunities each returning day. Help us to use these blessings to the best of our capacity, devoting ourselves to your service, and putting our selfish interests aside to seek the welfare of others. We pray in the Name of him who came among us as one who serves, Jesus Christ our Lord. **Amen.**[26]

C. Scripture Readings

1. For General Use

Old Testament
Exodus 15 (Song of Moses and Miriam)
Joshua 3:14–4:7 (Crossing over Jordan)

A SERVICE OF DEATH AND RESURRECTION

Job 14:1-12*a;* 19:25-27 (Man that is born of woman is of few days. . . . My Redeemer lives.)

Isaiah 25:1, 6-9; 26:1-4, 19 (God will swallow up death. . . . Thou wilt keep him in perfect peace whose mind. . . .)

Isaiah 61:1-4, 10-11 (The Spirit of the Lord is upon me. . . . Righteousness shall spring forth.)

Ezekiel 37:1-14, 21-28 (The valley of dry bones. . . . I will be their God.)

Psalms

27, 34, 40, 71, 77, 84, 118, 126

The Apocrypha

Wisdom 3:1-3, 5; 5:15-17 (The souls of the righteous are in the hand of God.)

Epistles

Acts 10:34-43 (Peter's sermon on Jesus' passion and resurrection)

Romans 5:1-11, 17-21 (We are justified by faith . . . grace, righteousness, eternal life.)

II Corinthians 5:1-11, 14-20 (Away from the body . . . at home in the Lord . . . in Christ a new creation.)

Ephesians 3:14-21 (I bow my knees to God . . . to know the love of Christ.)

Philippians 3:7-21 (That I may know the power of Christ's resurrection . . . I press on. . . . Christ will change our body.)

Colossians 3:1-17 (If you have been raised with Christ, seek the things that are above.)

I Thessalonians 4:13–5:11 (We would not have you ignorant concerning those who sleep.)

Hebrews 11, 12 (Faith . . . the saints)

Revelation 14:1-3, 6-7, 12-13 (The song of the redeemed. They rest from their labors.)

Revelation 21:1-7 (I saw a new heaven and a new earth.)

Gospels

Matthew 5:1-12 (The Beatitudes)

Matthew 25:31-46 (The Last Judgment. As you did it to one of the least of these. . . .)

Matthew 28:1-10, 16-20 (The open tomb. Go and make disciples.)

Mark 16:1-7 (The open tomb. He goes before you.)

Luke 12:22-40 (Be not anxious . . . be ready, for the Son of man comes.)

John 5:19-28 (Whoever hears my word and believes has eternal life.)

John 6:30-40, 47-51 (Feeding of the five thousand. I am the bread of life . . . eternal life.)

John 10:1-17 (The Good Shepherd)

John 12:20-36 (The hour has come. . . . Unless a grain of wheat dies. . . . Believe in the light.)

John 15:1-17 (The vine and the branches. Love one another.)

John 16:12-22, 33 (Promise of the Spirit . . . of joy. I have overcome the world.)

John 20 (Mary Magdalene at the empty tomb. Thomas.)

2. At the Service for a Child or Youth

Old Testament

Genesis 22:1-18 (Abraham and Isaac)

II Samuel 12:16-23 (David and the death of his child)

Isaiah 65:17-25 (I create a new heaven. . . . There shall be no more weeping . . . . An infant that lives but a few days. . . . The wolf and the lamb shall feed together.)

Lamentations 3:19-26, 31-33 (Remember my affliction. . . . The Lord is good.)

Joel 2:1, 12-13, 23-25a, 26-29 (I will pour out my Spirit. . . . Your sons and daughters shall see visions.)

Psalms

103:6-18 (As a father pities his children.)

Gospels

Matthew 11:25-30 (I thank thee thou has revealed these things to babes. . . . Take my yoke.)

Matthew 18:1-5, 10-14 (The child, the greatest in the kingdom.)

Matthew 19:13-15; Mark 10:13-16 (Let the children come to me.)

Mark 5:35-43; Matthew 9:18-19, 23-26 (Jesus' raising of the ruler's daughter)

3. An Untimely or Tragic Death

Old Testament

Lamentations 3:1-9, 19-26, 31-33 (I have seen affliction . . . wormwood and the gall . . . the Lord is good.)

Psalms

103 (Bless the Lord . . . who redeems from destruction.)

Epistles

Revelation 21:1-6; 22:1-5 (I saw a new heaven. . . . The former things are passed away. . . . The Lord God will be their light.)

Gospels

Mark 4:35-41 (Jesus' calming of the storm)

Luke 15:11-32 (The prodigal son)

John 6:35-40 (I am the bread of life. I will lose none. Eternal life.)

4. At the Service for the Non-Christian or Unchurched

Old Testament

Ecclesiastes 3:1-15 (For everything there is a season.)

Lamentations 3:1-9, 19-26 (I have seen affliction. . . . The Lord is good to those who wait on him.)

Psalms

39 (Lord, make me to know the measure of my days.)

The Apocrypha

Wisdom 3:1-3, 5; 5:15-17 (The souls of the righteous are in the hand of God.)

Epistles

Romans 14:7-13 (None lives to himself. Why do you pass judgment?)

Gospel

Matthew 5:1-12 (The Beatitudes)

Matthew 25:31-46 (As you did it to one of the least of these. . . .)

Luke 20:27-39 (God is not the God of the dead, but of the living.)

ADDITIONAL RESOURCES

D. Holy Communion

An alternative to "An Order for Holy Communion" in the service text, to be used when the congregation cannot participate in the prayer

Lift up your hearts and give thanks to the Lord our God.

Blessed are you, Lord our God,
  Creator and Sovereign of the Universe.
You loved the world so much
  you gave your only Son Jesus Christ to be our Saviour.
He suffered and died for the sin of the world,
  to free us from unending death.
You raised him victorious from the dead
  that we, too, might have new and everlasting life.
He ascended to be with you in glory
  and by the power of your Holy Spirit is with us always.
On the night he offered himself up for us
  he took bread, gave thanks to you, broke it, gave it to his
    disciples,
  and said: "Take, eat; this is my body which is given for you.
  Do this in remembrance of me."
When supper was over,
  he took the cup, gave thanks to you, gave it to his disciples,
  and said: "Drink from this, all of you;
  this cup is the new covenant sealed by my blood,
  poured out for you and many, for the forgiveness of sins.
  Whenever you drink it, do this in remembrance of me."
Therefore, in remembrance of all your mighty acts in Jesus
    Christ,
  we ask you to accept this our sacrifice of praise and
    thanksgiving,
  which we offer in union with Christ's offering for us,
  as a living and holy surrender of ourselves.
Send the power of your Holy Spirit on us and on these gifts,
  that the sharing of this bread and wine
    may be for us a sharing in the body and blood of Christ,

that we may be one body in him, cleansed by his blood,
and that we may faithfully serve him in the world,
  looking forward to his coming in final victory.
Renew our communion with all your saints,
  especially (*name*), and all those most dear to us.
May we run with perseverance the race that is set before us
  and with them receive the unfading crown of glory,
  through your Son Jesus Christ.
Through him, with him, and in him, in the unity of the Holy
  Spirit,
  we are made bold to pray the prayer that he has taught us.

The Service continues with the Lord's Prayer and the remainder of the Order.

E. Dismissals With Blessing

If then you have been raised with Christ, seek the things that are above where Christ is seated at the right hand of God. Set your mind on things that are above. For you have died and your life is hid with Christ in God. When Christ who is our life appears, then you also will appear with him in glory (Colossians 3:1-4). Grace to you and peace from God our Father (Colossians 1:2*b*). **Amen.**

May God who commanded the light to shine out of darkness, shine evermore in your hearts, to give the light of knowledge of the glory of God in the face of Jesus Christ (II Corinthians 4:6). Grace be with all who love our Lord Jesus Christ with love undying (Ephesians 6:24). **Amen.**

Now may our Lord Jesus Christ himself, and God our Father who loved us and gave us eternal comfort and good hope through grace, comfort your hearts and establish them in every good work and word (II Thessalonians 2:16). May the God of peace sanctify you wholly, that your spirit and soul and body be kept blameless until the coming of our Lord Jesus

Christ. The grace of the Lord Jesus Christ be with you (I Thessalonians 5:23, 28). **Amen.**

Fight the good fight of faith. Take hold of the eternal life to which you were called. And now to the blessed and only Sovereign, who alone has immortality and dwells in unapproachable light, be honor and dominion forever.(I Timothy 6:1a, 15b, 16a,c) **Amen.**

F. At the Committal Service

1. Committals

Into your hands, merciful God, we commend the soul of (*name*), as we commit _____ body to the ground, earth to earth, ashes to ashes, dust to dust, in sure and certain hope of life in the world to come; through our Lord Jesus Christ, who shall fashion anew our earthly body that it may be like unto his own glorious body, according to his mighty working whereby he is able to subdue all things unto himself.[27]

Unto you, almighty God, we commend the soul of (*name*), and to the elements we commit _____ body, in sure and steadfast faith that as _____ has borne the image of the earthly, so also _____ now bears the image of the heavenly.[28]

Unto the love of God we commend the soul of (*name*), and to the ground _____ body, earth to earth, ashes to ashes, dust to dust, praying that as _____ has borne the image of the earthly, so also _____ may bear the image of the heavenly.[29]

Almighty God, in whose eternal keeping are the souls of all your people, we commit these ashes of the body of (*name*) to the earth, in sure and certain faith that _____ spirit now lives with you, praying that you will have mercy upon _____, and that _____ may grow in your love and service forever more.[30]

God of us all, from whom we come and unto whom all souls return, we commit the mortal remains of (*name*) to their last resting place, in the faith that _____ is with you, and in the sure hope of resurrection to eternal life, through Jesus Christ who was dead and is alive forever more, and who holds the keys of the grave and of death.[31]

(*At a reinterment*) Eternal God, in whose holy keeping are the souls of those who love you, we commit again to its resting place the body of (*name*) departed; and we commend _____ soul to your merciful care, praying that you will continue your love and peace to _____, now and forever.[32]

---

2. Prayers

God of the dead and of the living, as we give (*name*) into your hands, so also we give into your heart our grief, our penitence for whatever more we might have been or done, and our love for _____ forever. Keep true in us the love in which we hold _____ and one another. And bring us with him face to face in your glory—your loving presence among us all, forever more. **Amen.**[33]

God, helper of the helpless, comfort our mourning hearts. In the knowledge that in your holy keeping are both the living and the dead, enable us to return to our duties and tasks. With chastened desires, with purer motives, with less trust in ourselves and more trust in you, may we serve your holy will, and henceforth live our lives in the spirit of him who was made perfect through suffering, Jesus Christ our Lord. **Amen.**[34]

O God, whose love for your people is from everlasting to everlasting, accept our prayers for your servant (*name*), and grant _____ entrance into your light and joy, in the communion of all your saints; through Jesus Christ our Lord. **Amen.**[35]

---

3. Dismissals with Blessing

Jesus said: "Peace I leave with you. My peace I give to you. Not as the world gives do I give to you. Let not your hearts be troubled, neither let them be afraid." The grace of the Lord Jesus Christ, and the love of God, and the fellowship of the Holy Spirit be with you all. **Amen.**

Notes

1. See Caryl Micklem, ed., *Contemporary Prayers for Public Worship* (Grand Rapids, Mich.: Eerdmans, 1967), pp. 17, 106. Used by permission.
2. See Caryl Micklem, ed., *More Contemporary Prayers* (Grand Rapids, Mich.: Eerdmans, 1970), pp. 3, 101. Used by permission.
3. Adapted by permission of Charles Scribner's Sons from *Prayers for Services* edited by Morgan Phelps Noyes. Copyright 1934 Charles Scribner's Sons; renewal copyright © 1962 Morgan Phelps Noyes. See p. 231.
4. See Karl Barth, *Selected Prayers*, p. 68, trans. by Keith R. Crim © M. E. Bratcher 1965. Used by permission of John Knox Press.
5. See Noyes, *Prayers,* p. 225.
6. See Protestant Episcopal Church in the U.S.A., Liturgical Commission, Prayer Book Studies 25, *Prayers, Thanksgivings and Litanies* (New York: Church Hymnal Corporation, 1973), p.81. Copyright 1973 by Charles Mortimer Guilbert as Custodian of the Standard Book of Common Prayer.
7. See Inter-Lutheran Commission on Worship for Provisional Use, *Contemporary Worship:* 10 © 1976 Concordia Publishing House. Used by permission.
8. See Joseph Buchanan Bernardin, comp., *Burial Services* (New York: Morehouse Gorham, 1941), p.58. Used by permission of Morehouse-Barlow.
9. See *ibid.,* p. 49.
10. Adapted by permission of Charles Scribner's Sons from *Prayers for a New World* edited by John Wallace Suter. Copyright © 1964 John W. Suter. See p. 194.
11. *The Book of Common Prayer, (Proposed),* copyright 1977 by Charles Mortimer Guilbert as Custodian of the Standard Book of Common Prayer (New York: Church Hymnal Corporation and Seabury Press), p. 99.
12. See Suter, *op. cit.,* p. 42.
13. See *ibid.,* p. 45.
14. See Protestant Episcopal Church, *Prayers, Thanksgivings and Litanies,* p. 154.
15. See James Dalton Morrison, comp. and ed., *Minister's Service Book* (Chicago: Willett, Clark & Company, 1937), pp. 222, 223; Noyes, p. 229.
16. See Bernardin, *Burial Services,* p. 64; Morrison, *Service Book,* p. 223.
17. See H. J. T. Bennett, *Prayers for the Sick, the Dying and the Departed* (Milwaukee: Morehouse Publishing Co., 1928), p. 81. Used by permission of Morehouse-Barlow.
18. Based on a prayer in O. Thomas Miles, *Dialogues with God* (Grand Rapids: Eerdmans Publishing Company, n. d.), p. 162.
19. See Walter Russell Bowie, *Lift Up Your Hearts* (Nashville, Abingdon Press, 1939, 1956).
20. See Morrison, *Service Book,* p. 215.
21. See Micklem, *More Prayers,* p. 15.
22. See Noyes, *Prayers,* p. 181.
23. See Bernardin, *Burial Services,* pp. 39, 40.
24. See *ibid.,* p.75.
25. See Theodore Parker Ferris, *Book of Prayer for Everyman* (New York: Seabury Press, 1962).

26. See Protestant Episcopal Church, *Prayers, Thanksgiving and Litanies,* p. 46.

27. See Bernardin, *Burial Services,* pp. 25-26.

28. See *ibid.,* p. 7.

29. See *ibid.,* p. 76.

30. See *ibid.,* p. 32.

31. See L. S. Hunter, ed., *A Diocesan Service Book* (London: Oxford University Press, 1965), p. 14. Used by permission of Oxford University Press (altered by permission).

32. See Bernardin, *Burial Services,* p. 32.

33. See *ibid.,* p. 29.

34. See *ibid.,* pp. 28-29.

35. See *ibid.,* p. 28.

A SERVICE OF DEATH AND RESURRECTION

CONCERNING THE SERVICE

The service should be held in the church if at all possible, and at a time when members of the congregation can be present.

This order is intended for use with the body of the deceased present, but it can be adapted for use at memorial services or other occasions.

The coffin remains closed throughout the service and thereafter. It may be covered with a pall.

Members of the deceased's family, friends, members of the congregation are strongly encouraged to share in conducting the service.

Optional parts of the service are in brackets [ ]. Parts in boldface type are to be said or sung by the people.

Part or all of the committal service may be included in the church service as indicated.

ORDER OF SERVICE

GATHERING OF THE PEOPLE

The pastor may welcome the family.

Music for worship may be offered while the people gather.

Songs of faith may be sung any time during the gathering.

If the coffin is already in place, the pastor opens the service with the following sentences. If not, it may be carried into the place of worship in procession, the pastor going before it and saying the sentences. The congregation stands.

THE WORD OF GRACE
Jesus said, I am the Resurrection and I am Life. Those who believe in me, even though they die, yet shall they live, and whoever lives and believes in me shall never die. I am Alpha and Omega, the beginning and the end, the first and the last. I died, and behold I am alive forever more, and I hold the keys of hell and death. Because I live, you shall live also.

GREETING
Friends, we have gathered here to praise God and to witness to our faith as we celebrate the life of (name). We come together in grief acknowledging our human loss. May God search our hearts, that in pain we may find comfort, in sorrow hope, in death resurrection.

The following sentences may be added immediately
after the Greeting if they have not been used
earlier at the placing of the pall on the coffin.

Dying, Christ destroyed our death.
Rising, Christ restored our life.
Christ will come again in glory.
As in baptism (name) put on Christ,
so in Christ may (name) be clothed with glory.
Here and now, dear friends, we are God's children.
What we shall be has not yet been revealed.
But we know that when he appears we shall be like
   him, for we shall see him as he is.
Those who have this hope purify themselves as Christ
   is pure.

HYMN OR SONG

PRAYER
The following or other prayers may be offered, in unison if desired. Petition for God's help, thanksgiving
for the communion of saints, confession of sin and assurance of pardon are appropriate here.

Pastor: The Lord be with you.
People: And also with you.

Pastor: Let us pray.
O God, who gave us birth,
you are ever more ready to hear than we are to pray.
You know our needs before we ask,
   and our ignorance in asking.
Give to us now your grace,
that as we shrink before the mystery of death
we may see the light of eternity.

Speak to us once more your solemn message of life
  and of death.
Help us to live as those who are prepared to die.
And when our summons comes,
may we die as those who go forth to live,
so that living or dying, our life may be in you,
and nothing in life or in death will be able
  to separate us
from your great love in Christ Jesus our Lord. Amen.

and/or

Eternal God, we praise you for the great company
of all those who have finished their course in faith
and now rest from their labor.
We praise you for those dear to us
whom we name in our hearts before you.
We praise you for your child (name),
whom you have taken to yourself.
Grant peace to their souls.
Let perpetual light shine upon them.
And help us so to believe where we have not seen,
that your presence may lead us through our years,
and bring us at last with them into the joy
  of your home
not made with hands but eternal in the heavens;
through Jesus Christ our Lord. Amen.

and/or

Holy God, before you our hearts are open
and from you no secrets are hidden.
We bring to you now our shame and sorrow
  for our sins.
We have forgotten that our life is from you
  and unto you.
We have neither sought nor done your will.

vi

We have not been truthful in our hearts,
in our speech, in our lives.
We have not loved as we ought to love.
Help us and heal us, we pray.
Raise us from our sins into a better life,
that we may end our days in peace
trusting in your kindness unto the end;
through Jesus Christ our Lord,
who lives and reigns with you
   in the unity of the Holy Spirit,
one God now and forever. Amen.

PARDON

Who is in a position to condemn?
Only Christ, Christ who died for us, who rose for us,
who reigns at God's right hand and prays for us.
Thanks be to God who gives us the victory
through our Lord Jesus Christ.

PSALM 130

Said or sung by the people, standing.

Out of the depths I cry unto thee, O Lord!
   Lord, hear my cry.
Let thine ears be attentive
   to the voice of my supplication.
If thou, Lord, should mark iniquities,
   Lord, who could stand?
But there is forgiveness with thee,
   that thou may be feared.
I wait for the Lord, my soul waits,
   and in his word do I hope.
My soul waits for the Lord
   more than those who watch for the morning.
O Israel, hope in the Lord!
   For with the Lord is great mercy.

With him is plenteous redemption,
   and he will redeem Israel from all their sins.

PROCLAMATION AND PRAISE

SCRIPTURE READINGS
Lections are from the Old and New Testaments. A short prayer for illumination may precede the lections. Preferably, a lection from one of the gospels should conclude the readings. It may be read from the midst of the congregation. Lay readers may be selected.

OLD TESTAMENT
(Arrangement of verses may be altered.)
Preferred:
Isaiah 40:1-6, 8-11, 28-31
Recommended:
Exodus 14:5-14, 19-31
Isaiah 43:1-3a, 5-7, 13, 15, 18-19, 25; 44:6, 8a
Isaiah 55:1-3, 6-13
Psalms 42, 43, 46, 90, 91, 103, 116, 121, 139, 145, 146
See alternative readings in Additional Resources.

PSALM 23
Sung or said by the people, standing.
The Lord is my Shepherd; I shall not want.
He maketh me to lie down in green pastures:
   he leadeth me beside the still waters.
He restoreth my soul:
   he leadeth me in the paths of righteousness
   for his name's sake.
Yea, though I walk through the valley of the shadow of death,
   I will fear no evil:

for thou art with me;
thy rod and thy staff they comfort me.
Thou preparest a table before me
in the presence of mine enemies:
thou anointest my head with oil:
my cup runneth over.
Surely goodness and mercy shall follow me
all the days of my life:
and I will dwell in the house of the Lord for ever.

EPISTLE
(Arrangement of verses may be altered.)
Preferred:
I Corinthians 15:1-8, 12-20, 35-44, 53-55, 57-58
Revelation 21:1-7, 22-27; 22:1-5
Recommended:
Romans 8:1-2, 5-6, 10-11, 14-19, 22-28, 31-32, 35-39
II Corinthians 4:5-18
Ephesians 1:15-23; 2:1, 4-10
I Peter 1:3-9, 13, 21-25
Revelation 7:2-3, 9-17
See alternative readings in Additional Resources.

GOSPEL
(Arrangement of verses may be altered.)
Preferred:
John 14:1-10a, 15-21, 25-27
Recommended:
Luke 24:13-35
John 11:1-5, 20-27, 32-35, 38-44
See alternative readings in Additional Resources.

SERMON
A brief sermon may be preached, proclaiming the gospel in the face of death. It may lead into, or include,

the following acts of naming and witness. These should
be concluded with a hymn.

NAMING
The life and death of the deceased may be gathered up
by the reading of a memorial or appropriate statement,
or in other ways, by the pastor or others.

WITNESS
Family, friends, members of the congregation may
briefly voice their thankfulness to God for the grace
they have received in the life of the deceased, and their
Christian faith and joy. Signs of faith, hope, and love
may be exchanged.

HYMN

OFFERING OF LIFE

If the Committal is to conclude this service, the Order
of Committal may be shortened and substituted for this
section.

CREED
The congregation, standing, may be led in the Apostles' Creed. If it has not been preceded by, it may be
followed by, a hymn or musical response.

**I believe in God, the Father almighty,
   creator of heaven and earth.**

**I believe in Jesus Christ, his only Son, our Lord.
He was conceived by the power of the Holy Spirit
   and born of the Virgin Mary.**

He suffered under Pontius Pilate,
    was crucified, died, and was buried.
He descended to the dead.
On the third day he rose again.
He ascended into heaven,
    and is seated at the right hand of the Father.
He will come again to judge the living and the dead.

I believe in the Holy Spirit,
    the holy catholic Church,
    the communion of saints,
    the forgiveness of sins,
    the resurrection of the body,
    and the life everlasting. Amen.

PRAYERS

The following or other prayers may be offered. They
may take the form of a pastoral prayer, a series of short-
er prayers, or a litany. Intercession, commendation of
life, and thanksgiving are appropriate here, concluded
with the Lord's Prayer.

God of us all, your love never ends.
When all else fails, you still are God.
We pray to you for one another in our need,
and for all, anywhere, who mourn with us this day.
To those who doubt, give light;
    to those who are weak, strength;
to all who have sinned, mercy;
    to all who sorrow, your peace.
Keep true in us the love with which we hold each other.
In all our ways we trust you.
And to you, with your Church on earth and in heaven,
we offer honor and glory, now and for ever. **Amen.**

O God, all that you have given us is yours.
As first you gave (name) to us
so now we give (name) back to you.

Here the pastor, with other celebrants, standing near
the coffin, may lay hands on it, continuing:

Receive (name) into the arms of your mercy.
Raise (name) up with all your people.
Receive us also, our selves, our souls, our bodies,
and raise us into a new life.
Help us so to love and serve you in this world
that we may enter into your joy in the world to come.
Amen.

HOLY COMMUNION

The pastor may administer the Sacrament to all present
who wish to share at the Lord's Table, using the Order
on page xv. Otherwise the service continues with the
following:

PRAYER OF THANKSGIVING

God of love, we thank you for all the happiness
with which you have blessed us even to this day:
for the gift of life; for home and friends;
for health and strength;
for work, and nature, and beauty;
for our baptism and place in your Church
    with all who have faithfully lived and died.
More than all else we thank you for Jesus
    who knew our griefs,
who died our death and rose for our sake,
and who lives and prays for us.
As he taught us, so now we pray.

THE LORD'S PRAYER

Our Father in heaven,
   hallowed be your Name,
   your kingdom come,
   your will be done,
   on earth as in heaven.
Give us today our daily bread.
Forgive us our sins
   as we forgive those
   who sin against us.
Save us from the time of trial,
   and deliver us from evil.
For the kingdom, the power,
   and the glory are yours,
   now and for ever. Amen.

or

Our Father, who art in heaven,
   hallowed be thy Name,
   thy kingdom come,
   thy will be done,
   on earth as it is in heaven.
Give us this day our daily bread.
And forgive us our trespasses,
   as we forgive those
   who trespass against us.
And lead us not into temptation,
   but deliver us from evil.
For thine is the kingdom,
   and the power, and the glory,
   forever. Amen.

HYMN

DISMISSAL AND BLESSING

The pastor, facing the people, may say one or more of the following, or other words of dismissal and blessing.

Now may the God of Peace
who brought again from the dead our Lord Jesus,
the great Shepherd of the sheep,
by the blood of the eternal covenant,
equip you with everything good
   that you may do his will,
working in you that which is pleasing in his sight,
through Jesus Christ;
   to whom be glory for ever and ever. **Amen.**

The peace of God which passes all understanding
keep your hearts and minds
   in the knowledge and love of God,
and of his Son Jesus Christ our Lord.
And the blessing of God almighty,
the Father, Son, and Holy Spirit,
be among you and remain with you always. **Amen.**

Now may the Father
from whom every family in heaven and on earth
   is named,
according to the riches of his glory,
grant you to be strengthened with might
through his Spirit in your inner being,
that Christ may dwell in your hearts through faith;
that you, being rooted and grounded in love,
may be able to comprehend with all the saints
what is the breadth and length and height and depth,
and to know the love of Christ
   which surpasses knowledge,
   that you may be filled with all the fullness of God.

Now to him who by the power at work in us
is able to do far more abundantly
    than all we ask or think,
to him be glory in the church and in Christ Jesus
to all generations, for ever and ever. **Amen.**

RECESSIONAL

AN ORDER FOR HOLY COMMUNION

This may be included following the prayers on page xii
in the Order of Service, or before a common meal following the service, or with the family at some time
following the service. If included, it replaces the Prayer
of Thanksgiving and the Lord's Prayer, on page xii.

The bread and wine are brought to the table, or un-
covered if already in place. The pastor makes any necessary preparation of the elements and then prays the
following or another version of the Great Thanksgiving:

Pastor: The Lord be with you.
People: **And also with you.**
Pastor: Lift up your hearts.
People: **We lift them to the Lord.**
Pastor: Let us give thanks to the Lord our God.
People: **It is right to give him thanks and praise.**

Pastor:
Creator and Sovereign of the universe,
it is right that we should always and everywhere
give you thanks and praise,
through Jesus Christ our Lord,
who rose victorious from the dead,

and comforts us with the blessed hope of
   everlasting life.
For your faithful people life is changed, not ended;
and when our mortal body lies in death,
there is prepared for us a dwelling place
   eternal in the heavens.

Therefore, with your people in all ages
   and the whole company of heaven,
      we join in the song of unending praise.

Pastor and people:
Holy, holy, holy Lord, God of power and might,
heaven and earth are full of your glory.
   Hosanna in the highest.
Blessed is he who comes in the name of the Lord.
   Hosanna in the highest.

Pastor:
Blessed are you, Lord our God,
because you loved the world so much
   you gave your only Son Jesus Christ to be our Savior.
He suffered and died for the sin of the world.
You raised him from the dead
   that we, too, might have new life.
He ascended to be with you in glory,
   and by the power of your Holy Spirit
      is with us always.

On the night he offered himself up for us
he took bread, gave thanks to you, broke it,
   gave it to his disciples, and said:
"Take, eat; this is my body which is given for you.
   Do this in remembrance of me."

xvi

When supper was over,
he took the cup, gave thanks to you,
  gave it to his disciples, and said:
"Drink from this, all of you;
  this cup is the new covenant sealed by my blood,
  poured out for you and many,
  for the forgiveness of sins.
Whenever you drink it, do this in remembrance of me."

Therefore,
  in remembrance of all your mighty acts
  in Jesus Christ,
we ask you to accept
  this our sacrifice of praise and thanksgiving,
  which we offer in union with Christ's offering for us
  as a living and holy surrender of ourselves.

Send the power of your Holy Spirit on us
  and on these gifts,
that the sharing of this bread and wine
  may be for us a sharing
  in the body and blood of Christ,
that we may be one body in him, cleansed by his blood,
and that we may faithfully serve him in the world,
  looking forward to his coming in final victory.

Renew our communion with all your saints,
  especially (name) and all those most dear to us.
May we run with perseverance the race that is set
  before us
  and with them receive the unfading crown of glory,
  through your Son Jesus Christ.

Through him, with him, and in him,
   in the unity of the Holy Spirit,
all glory and honor is yours, almighty God,
   now and for ever. Amen.

Our Father in heaven,
   hallowed be your Name,
   your kingdom come,
   your will be done,
   on earth as in heaven.
Give us today our daily bread.
Forgive us our sins
   as we forgive those
   who sin against us.
Save us from the time of trial,
   and deliver us from evil.
For the kingdom, the power,
   and the glory are yours,
   now and for ever. Amen.
or
Our Father, who art in heaven,
   hallowed be thy Name,
   thy kingdom come,
   thy will be done,
   on earth as it is in heaven.
Give us this day our daily bread.
And forgive us our trespasses,
   as we forgive those
   who trespass against us.
And lead us not into temptation,
   but deliver us from evil.
For thine is the kingdom,
   and the power, and the glory,
   forever. Amen.

The pastor breaks the bread.

The bread and wine are given to the people with these or other words being exchanged:

The body of Christ, given for you. Amen.
The blood of Christ, given for you. Amen.

During the giving of the bread and wine, hymns or songs of praise may be sung.

Then follows the Dismissal and Blessing, on page xiv.

AN ORDER OF COMMITTAL

This service is intended primarily for burial in the ground. However, it can be adapted for cremation or the interment of ashes, for burial above ground or at sea, or when the body is donated for medical purposes.

The pastor should preside.

Prayers and lections appropriate for a service for a child or youth, or for other distinctive occasions are found in Additional Resources.

When the people have gathered, the pastor says one or more of the following:

In the midst of life we are in death;
from whom can we seek help?
Our help is in the name of the Lord,
who made heaven and earth.

He who raised Jesus Christ from the dead
will give life to your mortal bodies also
through his Spirit which dwells in you.

Behold, I tell you a mystery!
We shall not all die, but we shall all be changed.
This perishable nature must put on the imperishable,
this mortal the immortal.
Then shall come to pass the saying,
"Death is swallowed up in victory."
"O death, where is your sting?
O grave, where is your victory?"
Thanks be to God who gives us the victory
through our Lord Jesus Christ.

Therefore my heart is glad and my spirit rejoices.
My body also shall rest in hope.
You, Lord, will show me the path of life.
In your presence is fullness of joy,
and at your right hand are pleasures forever more.

The following prayer is offered:
Let us pray.
O God, you have ordered this wonderful world
   and know all things in earth and in heaven.
Give us such faith that by day and by night,
at all times and in all places,
we may without fear commit ourselves
   and those dear to us
to your never-failing love,
in this life and in the life to come. **Amen.**

One of the following or other Scriptures may be read:

Blessed be the God and Father of our Lord Jesus Christ! By his great mercy we have been born anew to a living hope through the resurrection of Jesus Christ from the dead, and to an inheritance which is imperishable, undefiled and unfading, kept in heaven for you. In this you rejoice, though now for a little while you may have to suffer various trials so that the genuineness of your faith may prove itself worthy at the revelation of Jesus Christ. Without having seen him, yet you love him; though you do not now see him, you believe in him and rejoice with unutterable and exalted joy. As the outcome of your faith you obtain the salvation of your souls.

Jesus said: The hour has come for the Son of man to be glorified. Truly, truly, I say to you, unless a grain of wheat falls into the earth and dies, it remains alone; but if it dies it bears much fruit. He who loves his life loses it, and he who hates his life in this world will keep it unto life eternal. If anyone serves me, he must follow me; and where I am, there shall my servant be also. If anyone serves me, the Father will honor him.

Standing at the head of the coffin and facing it, while earth is cast upon it as the coffin is lowered into the grave, the pastor says the following:
Almighty God, into your hands we commend your child (name), in sure and certain hope of resurrection to eternal life through Jesus Christ our Lord. **Amen.**

This body we commit to the ground (or the elements, or its resting place, or the deep), earth to earth, ashes to ashes, dust to dust. Blessed are the dead who die in the Lord. Henceforth, says the Spirit, they rest from their labors and their works follow them.

One or more of the following or other prayers is offered:

Let us pray.
Gracious God,
we thank you for those we love but see no more.
Receive into your arms your servant (name),
and grant that increasing in knowledge and love of you,
(name) may go from strength to strength
in service in your heavenly kingdom;
through Jesus Christ our Lord. **Amen.**

Almighty God,
look with pity upon the sorrow of your servants.
for whom we pray.
Help them amidst things they cannot understand
to trust in your care.
Bless them and keep them.
Make your face to shine upon them
and be gracious to them.
Lift up your countenance upon them
and give them peace. **Amen.**

O God, whose days are without end,
make us deeply aware of the shortness and uncertainty
of our human life.
Raise us from sin into love and goodness,
that when we depart this life we may rest in Christ
and receive the blessing he has promised
to those who love and serve him,
"Come, you blessed of my Father, receive the kingdom
prepared for you from the foundation of the world."
Grant this, merciful Father,
through Jesus Christ our Mediator and Redeemer.
   Amen.